A CHALLENGE TO
CHANGE

A CHALLENGE TO CHANGE

Beechy and Josephine Colclough

Thorsons
An Imprint of HarperCollins*Publishers*

Thorsons
An Imprint of HarperCollins*Publishers*
77–85 Fulham Palace Road
Hammersmith, London W6 8JB

The Thorsons website address is www.thorsons.com

Published by Thorsons 1999

1 3 5 7 9 10 8 6 4 2

A catalogue record for this book is available from the British Library

ISBN 0 7225 3814 6

Printed and bound in Great Britain by
Caledonian International Book Manufacturing Ltd, Glasgow

CONTENTS

ACKNOWLEDGEMENTS

We would like to thank all the therapists and clients who have so generously shared their ideas and experiences with us.

INTRODUCTION

ABOUT THIS BOOK

A Challenge To Change is an inspirational workbook aimed at people who have reached a watershed in their lives and need both the tools and the motivation, and most importantly the belief, to move on and make changes. This book will enable you to identify clearly and confront the areas in your life with which you are unhappy and discontented. Change requires both courage and insight. You know that there is no point in dreaming unless you really want those dreams to become a reality. So don't jump from dreaming to telling yourself what could get in the way. Stop that from being an automatic response. From now on, every time you think 'if only', we want you to stop and replace it with 'when'. Every time you feel sorry for yourself or go into 'negative mode', we want you to stop again and tell yourself that you will never move on unless you 'stop' being negative and 'start' believing that things can be different. This is an important key – to change you need to believe it is possible (even if you don't think you know how).

We are not trying to negate your feelings. What we are pointing out is that the way you think and see yourself are crucial ingredients to the formula that will either keep you stuck or will propel you forwards. From this moment you have a choice, and it is a very positive one if you allow it to be. Remember that at all times. Change begins with a decision and you have to support that decision by thinking positively, believing in yourself and acting 'as if'...

So from now on you don't have to be afraid to admit that things need to change. This is not a sign of weakness – it is a sign that you have the courage needed to make changes and the insight to recognize them. As soon as you do this, you will find that acceptance becomes the source of energy which will help you move on and enter the next phase of achieving the goals you have set. This book will help you look at what you want and need, and tell you how to avoid getting stuck in that rut of never realizing your goals. We don't accept, by the way, that you don't know what you need to do. What will be blocking you is the fear of admitting that things need to change because you may not know exactly what the solution is. Again, this book will help you, because it will give you the confidence to realize that you don't necessarily need to have a solution in order to accept that there needs to be change. You are not expected to have all the answers straightaway. Let yourself off that hook.

PREPARING YOURSELF FOR CHANGE

To start preparing yourself, we want you to think very specifically about how satisfied you are with your life. Do not be afraid of confronting this. There is absolutely nothing wrong with wanting to change things for the better. Change does not have to be about negating everything and starting from scratch. To begin to explore this area, ask yourself four key questions:

1 Does the outcome really meet with your expectations? To be plain, is this what you wanted?
2 What does your lifestyle cost? This is measured very broadly in terms of time pressures, effects on your mental and physical health (such as anxiety, depression, stress), relationships, spiritual life and, of course, finances. Be blunt – is the price too high? If it is then something needs to change. Don't sacrifice your mental and physical wellbeing. It just isn't worth it.
3 What are your priorities in life (your real ones, not ones that you think you should have)? Are you currently close to achieving

these or have you compromised them? Do you find it hard to balance work and time for yourself and others (work being a broad term to cover looking after others as well as paid employment)? Remember, also, that priorities change and you need to give yourself permission to explore that possibility.

4 Are there major problem areas in your life such as health problems, mental illness such as depression, relationship problems (with your spouse, partner, children, relatives), work crises?

Stop for just one moment. Put the book down. If you were brutally honest for one second, what do you *feel* needs to change? Again, we are not suggesting you should have the solution – just answer the question, then keep your answer in mind as you work through the book. Simon, a 29-year-old City broker, answered:

The first thought that came into my head was that I have a wife and baby I hardly see. I want to change that. I feel miserable a lot of the time but I don't know what I can do.

On a completely different level, you also need to address the issue of where your self-worth comes from. First, do you know what that really is? It is now such a buzz word that it may have become quite meaningless. Ask yourself what makes you feel literally 'of value'. What do you need to feel valued and worthy? People so often push themselves into careers because of the power and status they afford, as well as the financial rewards. There is absolutely nothing wrong with that if it works for you. Having said that, you also need to think about the sources from which you derive your positive feelings. Do you depend too much on one area such as work or money? Do you therefore tend to look to external sources and ignore the internal? As a result, do you leave your personal life to run itself? Think some more about extending your repertoire of resources. Being driven by your career or money may work for a short time but where does that leave you?

HELP YOURSELF

Have you ever asked yourself why self-help books have become so popular? They are fulfilling a need – people today are constantly struggling to find meaning in their lives. Some of you picked up this book because you are looking for a sense of direction – this can be personally, professionally, spiritually, socially, physically or educationally. This book can help you explore such issues.

In the last few decades we have heard more and more about stress. You can work hard and put in long hours if you feel there is a point – stress hits when people feel stuck on a treadmill, and life becomes an interminable process of desperately trying to reach the finishing line. It is important to make sure that you feel there is a point to what you are doing in your life and to reassess it. After all, your priorities do change, and there will be many an ambitious person who reaches 35–40 and simply feels that they are no longer driven by what drove them in their 20s. This can come as a terrible shock. Sometimes people need to be able to re-evaluate the direction in which they are going. The expression 'opting out' refers to people who stop conforming – what an emotive two words to describe people who have the courage to confront the fact that they are troubled by what to do with their lives. If you give up an executive position because you are truly unhappy and do something completely different, such as starting a smallholding, are you 'opting out' or are you simply in contact with what is driving you? Has it changed? Is it just time to do something different rather than staying stuck on a treadmill that is quite possibly making you physically and mentally ill?

At different stages in your life you will quite naturally flirt with the notion of a need to change. You will often stay at that flirtation level of thinking and picturing and mulling over, but go no further. Your desire for change can be about something serious or something less significant. It can be wanting to get fit or to break a negative habit, such as an addiction to drugs, alcohol, food, gambling or even shopping; it can be a change of career, reassessing a relationship, the issue of whether to have children or not, the need to get help with a psychological or medical problem. The list goes on and on...

The key question is: why do you have these conversations with yourself and simply go no further with them? What is it you need to do differently to propel yourself forwards so that you can move out of that contemplation phase and into action? What are the barriers that you tend to build? All of this will be explored in greater depth so that you can become aware of the traps you make for yourself and what needs to be done in order to achieve a different outcome. Wouldn't it be exciting to believe that things don't have to stay dreams? How frustrated do you get with yourself when you have to own up to the fact that you get excited about change and then do nothing about it? What energy would you really have available to make those changes if you knew that you really could do it and that they were going to last?

In contemplating this it is very important to be realistic, but don't set your sights too low either. You need to find the balance between being realistic and tipping the scales by being overly negative. We can hear you saying 'how can I tell which is which?'. There is no easy answer, but by talking to other people and checking things out you can start to move towards some sort of an answer. We also suggest that you don't try to 'move mountains'. We believe that small changes will have a knock-on effect, so start making small changes and wait and see what the impact is. This strategy will also help you maintain changes because you are not dealing with anything that you are not going to be able to manage.

OBSTACLES TO SUCCESS

Fear and Anxiety

How aware are you of your own hurdles of fear, lack of self-esteem and confidence? Have you fallen into that trap of deciding that they are a characteristic that is simply a part of you and cannot, therefore, be changed. *A Challenge to Change* helps you challenge this notion and teaches you to be aware of your many options. You will learn that hurdles have two sides. They obviously exist for a reason but sometimes you take them that bit too far, and then they start to interfere and get in the way. Take fear, for example. It is perfectly sensible and helpful to feel fear if you are trapped in a room where a fire has broken out. In day-to-day life, however, fear can stop you doing the things you would really love to do. The same is true of anxiety. You all probably recognize that stomach-churning feeling, teamed with sweating palms and a tightness in the chest. Again, there are two sides to anxiety. One thing that is usually completely ignored is that anxiety is about really wanting something. Think about it – if you go for an interview or sit an exam, what is it you are really anxious about? Don't tell us that you are anxious about failing – no, the anxiety lies in the desire to be successful, but it can have such a negative effect. So, the next time you are anxious, don't focus on the unpleasant symptoms. Instead, start to energize yourself by asking 'what is it I want?'. We will speak more about this later on in the book.

The Past

Another very common hurdle for people is 'the past'. Without a doubt, you are shaped by your life experiences, but they don't need to rule you completely. Isn't it such an exciting thought that you can decide not to be a powerless victim but someone who can take your power in a healthy way – you can become the sculptor of your life rather than being trapped by something that was handed on to you. If you have had problems in your early life, we know that they can never be made to go away, but we always say to people that what is important is not to have to keep paying the price. Once was enough – don't let your life be ruined forever. Have the courage to move forwards. It does not mean that whatever happened doesn't matter but acknowledges that it is time to get on with your life and that you deserve some good in it. You cannot remove or change the past but you can fill today with some positives.

Negative Self-talk

The way you talk to yourself can be a hurdle. Think about it: your head is never silent; you are thinking all of the time, and a lot of the time you are saying things to yourself. It is so important to become more aware of the messages you give yourself. You may not always be aware of where all the messages come from. Sometimes they are influenced by what significant people have said to you, e.g. your parents, teachers, peers – these people so obviously shape us that you can sometimes listen to them too much, and carry on saying things to yourself that simply don't apply. Sometimes messages come from experiences; something may happen just once and you 'generalize' that experience, that is you link things together in a concrete cause-and-effect way. For example, some people will be put off applying for a promotion because they have been turned down once before. They end up saying to themselves 'there's no point, that sort of thing doesn't happen to me'. What a damning statement! We are sure that you can think of lots of messages that you give yourself. Here are some examples:

- I'm not a lucky person.
- It's pointless trying because I won't get anywhere.
- People like me just don't get that sort of promotion.
- I'm terrible at interviews.
- I've always wanted to do ... but I know I wouldn't be any good.
- I love playing sport but I don't think I should do it because I'm no good.
- I would like to try [xxxxx] but I think I would end up looking a fool.
- I can never be happy.

We will look at these messages with you in more depth later on in the book. If you can think of some of your own now, just write them down and keep them for later.

GREAT EXPECTATIONS

Think also about expectations. Don't you think we expect too much of ourselves and others? We live in a world of opportunities but not all of us will get to experience them. What does that do? We often live with a hunger that can never be satisfied except for the 'chosen few'. But what is it you really want? Are you becoming a victim of too many choices rather than an agent of what you really want and *can* achieve? These are very important things to think about.

Contentment

How do you feel when you come up against someone who is truly content? Contentment is a state of mind that some people achieve, and it is priceless. Remember that happiness can only be achieved when your expectations meet reality. Perhaps sometimes we need to re-examine our expectations if they hardly ever meet reality rather than being angry and discontent with reality. Contentment, therefore, is something that comes from within. We can 'reorganize' our perspectives and expectations to achieve this.

Acceptance and Peace of Mind

It is important to think about and pinpoint what you want to change, but not to waste energy pursuing the impossible. One major goal that should be mentioned at this stage is the goal of acceptance, one which today's world does little to nurture. This book is not about achieving the goal of perfection; it is about making more of your life in all sorts of different ways – big and small.

HOW THIS BOOK CAN HELP YOU

A Challenge To Change will help guide you in terms of developing both a greater understanding and the skills to deal more effectively with your emotions, feelings and relationships. Some of the most important experiences in your life are those that you are ill-prepared for. What have you really been taught about relationships? Probably hardly anything at all. Who sits you down and tells you that it is OK to have feelings? How many of you have been shown that it is OK to ask for help or to express feelings of depression or negativity? This book will give you permission to do some of this differently. It is also important to know that other people often feel the same – but if you are not expressing it to anyone else you will never know. Through some of the exercises in this book you will start to become more sensitive to how others in your life are likely to 'see' you and their world, and they could prove to be useful stepping stones in starting to communicate in a different and more meaningful way. Solving relationship problems is never about who is right or wrong. It is about finding a way forward. This happens when you take time to understand each other.

Think about just how emotionally isolated you are. Yes, you are surrounded by people, but on what level do you communicate? Men can be the biggest culprits. Many have been taught that men don't discuss 'weaknesses', and often suffer needlessly. We hope that this book will leave you with a very strong message that feelings are nothing to do with weakness and that it takes a strong person to be able to discuss problems openly.

People often consider change in their lives after a crisis. Think about bereavement for a second and the impact it has today. We really don't accept the inevitability or commonness of death any more – we expect so much of modern medicine, miracles even. We also no longer experience death at close hand – it is sanitized and kept at a distance. Anger is such a key part of the grieving process, and a lot of that anger is about coming to terms with the fact that the deceased has left you behind. We often ask 'couldn't more have been done?'. This can be directed towards the medical staff or to ourselves, that is should we have done more? Our first experiences of bereavement are also bound to make us question our perspectives and goals.

Problems in relationships can be crisis points in our lives. People may be marrying later, but there are still many people in their 30s and 40s who are struggling to come to terms with divorce and separation. Because it is so common, it appears that it is something that people are expected to 'get over'. As a result of broken relationships, many fathers are forced to live away from their children. Fathers who try to maintain regular contact often find that they cannot easily divide their lives, and suffer as a result. In the same way, many women are bringing children up on their own, and because it is almost accepted that women cope with this, they are often given very little emotional and physical support.

Another potential crisis area is our career. People in their late 30s are aware that the 40s are an era that is highlighted as the beginning of the end! This is a fairly new phenomenon. What is it like in your mid 30s to be facing this? What is it like to be classified in this way when you are probably entering a phase in your life of greater confidence and self-esteem only to have the carpet pulled from underneath you? What does this do?

As you can see, *A Challenge To Change* will help you address many issues on the subject of change. It is possible to do this because it will explore these areas from a feelings perspective. The book is organized into three sections:

1 The first section consists of the first six chapters. These are designed for you to begin to explore and understand your personality and make-up and what is going on in your life. You will be guided by sets of different exercises which will help you to clarify certain key points and thus gain greater insight.
2 The middle section is about how to make changes, and consists of the next four chapters.
3 The final section is about empowering yourself and thus consolidating the changes you have made.

Each chapter will contain useful exercises that need time and thought put into them to ensure the best results. It is also important to keep some sort of diary where you should record things such as your goals and keep a note of how things are progressing. The exercises should be repeated over time. We recommend that you read the book in its entirety, but if you prefer, you can speed-read certain parts.

When you work on any of the exercises in the book, it is a good idea to go to a special place to do them. It will help you in several ways – you will be hopefully choosing somewhere comfortable and without distractions, and it will also become somewhere that you associate with what you are doing. Just thinking about that place or going to it will help you be re-stimulated into forging ahead with what you are trying to achieve. It can almost be like a trigger that 'puts you in the mood' for the next task ahead. Also remember that you may need to allow your brain to 'incubate' some of the things that you are considering. If no helpful thoughts emerge immediately, do not worry – they will come eventually if you start the process of setting your mind into action mode. The possibilities are endless and should be so.

One of the key tools and major themes of this book is 'spotting your drivers'. Start by simply asking yourself the question 'what drives me?'. There are many layers to be explored and revealed in answering this question, and you need to be patient in moving through the levels to find the real answer. Remember that 'what drives you' can be positive or negative. It can propel you forwards or drive you back. In time you will discover the key to the more productive drivers, but at the beginning you need to become more aware. Your drivers will be created by your ambitions and aspirations, and on a deeper level they are created by your feelings, experiences and thought patterns. On a feeling level, a lot of you will be drawn to listen to and be directed by your negative drivers, such as fear, anxiety, low self-esteem, but this book will push you to be in contact with the many different drivers within you. It may even be that some drivers you have perceived as negative can be used quite productively, but you have never been aware of how to do this. Anxiety is a good example, because its positive side is about really wanting something. By doing this you will open up whole new areas that will expose you to greater and wider opportunities – personally, professionally, emotionally and spiritually. When you use your drivers in a positive manner they become this incredible source of energy and 'drive'. You know the difference between the energy required to do something that has a desired goal and one of which you have perhaps lost sight.

This book will challenge you to change your life for the better. It is a workbook and a thinking book. If you approach the exercises in this book honestly and truthfully, you will succeed in becoming more fulfilled. You have untapped resources and pools of energy. These are your positive drivers. If you are really heading in the right direction, the task ahead will seem effortless. Stress comes into our lives only when we are constantly pushing in a direction that is simply not appropriate for us, or does not make sense. Be excited about rediscovering that bountiful supply of energy and enthusiasm that is within you all.

PLEASE BE AWARE

We want you to promise yourself that you will seek further help and support if you feel the need for it. This book is no substitute for having one-to-one help which may be appropriate for certain issues. You need to use your judgement on this.

Also, if you are considering any type of changes concerning your health – mental or physical – you should consult your GP.

If you wish to find further help for specific problems, the Resources section at the back of the book may be able to guide you in the right direction.

What Do You Want to Change?

CHAPTER 1

It's Hard to Let Go When You're Still Holding On

Before you can really rise to the challenge of change you need to be aware of what may be holding you back, and deal with these issues and areas first. Change will be a lot less taxing if you are not battling with, or sabotaging, yourself, whether consciously or subconsciously. So ask yourself what anchors may be holding you back and keeping you from moving on. Be aware that anchors may well create a sense of safety because they are familiar (which can be confusing), but on closer inspection they reveal themselves as a hindrance to change – pure and simple. By getting rid of the obstacles that hold you back you can start to move in a more precise and positive direction, and not lose energy along the way. If you are unclear as to what anchors may be getting in your way, look at the list below and remember that anchors take many guises:

Types of Anchor

1 Internal processes – your internal dialogue and decision-making strategies.

2 Patterns and habits that you have created – 'this is how I have always done it'.

3 Perfectionism – 'I can only change if I do it perfectly'.

4 Guarantee required – 'I will only change if the results are guaranteed'.

5 Practical issues such as your responsibilities, duties, time constraints, current lifestyle.

6 Emotional states, such as fear and anxiety.

7 The no-luck anchor – almost like a superstition.

8 The physically tangible anchor, such as clutter and disorganization.

9 The no solution anchor – so stay in the familiar.

10 The mountains anchor – but changes can be made in stages so don't set out to climb a mountain all in one go – set yourself tasks that are possible to complete.

11 Can't see the future.

12 Security at any price.

13 Change feels stressful and is therefore mistaken as a warning sign not to proceed.

We will deal with these anchors in more detail further on in this chapter.

When we talk about letting go of anchors we are not talking about your becoming reckless or disregarding your responsibilities; that is simply another, and very negative, way of not allowing yourself to change. You sabotage yourself by making the experience of change as negative and harrowing as possible, or you frighten yourself by conjuring up the most terrifying pictures of what 'will' happen, or you convince yourself that so much has to change that it is just impossible to move forwards.

START NOW TO BECOME AWARE OF YOUR OWN PERSONAL ANCHORS

Let's get straight into a short exercise that will help you to continue to develop a deeper awareness of what exactly happens when you think about change in whatever shape or form that takes.

Put the book down now and think back to the last time you considered a change, and get acquainted with what happened. Try to choose the most recent example so that you can go through what happened very precisely.

Take Nicky as an example. She was thinking of changing her work schedule. She is self-employed but finds that she is working longer and longer hours:

When I think about not working so late I feel a tremendous sense of relief and excitement. I can actually picture myself at home doing 'normal' things that I miss – sitting in the garden on a summer's evening, watching TV – and I get really excited.

Then I flip into my 'insecure head' – 'suppose I lose clients?', 'what about the money?', 'shouldn't I do the work while it is there in case it dries up?'. At this stage I feel anxious and scared and the 'screen' is blank. I just hear these thoughts in my head like a radio play.

One very striking thing about Nicky is that, when she was thinking positively, she actually pictured herself, and this was a powerful tool to fuel her enthusiasm and positive feelings. When she began to think negatively she was more aware of an internal voice (quite a huge anchor for her) which makes her stay stuck even though she is unhappy. At this point – the point of no change – the screen is blank for Nicky. She is no longer contemplating change so there is nothing to move on towards.

Go back to your own example. When you have run through your own experience, ask yourself the following question: did you think about the positives or negatives first, or go from one to the other?

Part of this process reflects your natural decision-making style. Once you have made a decision, however, you need to keep focusing on the positives, the reasons why you are doing what you are doing, and the benefits of the change. The negatives don't have to be ignored (that would be ridiculous – but let them sit more comfortably on the sidelines rather than giving them too much power – we will talk more about this later).

To understand your strategy further, did you:

- Think in pictures like Nicky – seeing what you were thinking about like a video playing in your head or a picture album? How did this affect your feelings? Did it, for example, strengthen your positive feelings? Did your level of excitement grow?
- Or did you play the situation through in your mind hearing the words that would be spoken (almost like a radio play)?
- Or does this 'radio play' consist of your own internal dialogue?
- Or do you think about a particular scenario and start to experience the feelings that go with it?
- Or do you experience a combination of these elements?

Whatever it is that you do, start to get even more aware of it because it will be the first important key to moving forwards and keeping going. When you play that 'video' or 'radio play', be it in words, pictures or feelings, this is the first vital step in getting motivated. When you begin to falter, then is the time to 'play it again' and allow yourself to re-experience the positive feelings, thoughts, messages and pictures and stay motivated.

Most times when people consider changes – be they in a career, lifestyle, relationship, whatever – they will at some stage experience feelings of excitement and exhilaration. These, however, often change very quickly into feelings of fear, anxiety and negativity. As we have shown, people often increase the intensity of those feelings, positive and negative, by imagining themselves, picturing themselves, hearing themselves, feeling the feelings of what it would feel like 'if'. All of this is the start of such an important process which, nine times out of ten, will go no further. Why? There can be many reasons for this. Let's elaborate on some of the pointers raised at the beginning of this chapter.

FEAR

Fear is one of the most commonly used barriers to moving on. To understand the barrier you need to understand exactly what fear is. It is spelled **F E A R** which is an acronym for 'False Evidence Appearing Real'. Think about it for a moment. If we feel fear about something in the future we often create the scenario, picture it or feel it as if it were real, or as if it were actually going to happen. Say, for example, you have had an argument with a key figure at work. They are in a senior position to you. You go home that evening and start to get afraid about what will happen. You start to play certain scenarios through. 'Supposing I go to work tomorrow and get the sack? Supposing this person starts to run me down to other people?' The list of projections is as endless as it is negative. All of this is 'false evidence appearing real' but it is so powerful that it will start to affect how you feel, and as a result it influences what you do.

Remember that your thoughts drive how you feel. If you are worrying about something that currently hasn't happened and may not happen, then you are using that 'false evidence' in a very destructive way. As you well know, your fears often do not become reality but you can be ruled by that fear. So start to develop more of a sense of the 'false evidence' that you collect that actually just ends up getting in your way. Stop being influenced by something that simply has not happened. Stop living in the dread of what 'may' happen and start to concentrate more on today – the only day that you have any real influence over.

THE SECURITY TRAP

We also tend to hold on to what we have, what is familiar to us. It becomes the lifejacket which is actually so ungainly that we can't move in it. Think about it: people float well in lifejackets but they don't swim very far in them. They also have to wait for someone to come and rescue them. Often people convince themselves that it is better to stick with what they have; others go that one step further and tell themselves that the grass is never greener for them. So their fate is carved in stone. This technique leads people to contemplate change and then build a case against why it would be possible. They end up clutching that good old protector that will simply shield them from the opportunity to change.

SEEING THE FUTURE

There are also some people who have great difficulty 'seeing' the future. This makes moving forward extremely frightening and also very difficult. It must be like driving in the dark without any headlights – creating a sense of danger and a total inability to see where you are going! Don't give into this. If the screen for the future is blank you need to make a big effort to work on creating some things to move forward towards. It doesn't matter how small you start, just as long as you make that start. You will have difficulty moving forward if you let that 'screen' remain blank. If you can't think what you 'want', we are sure that you will be able to list what you 'don't want'. Take Philip as an example. He feels dissatisfied with his current relationship. He has difficulty saying what he is looking for in a new relationship, but when asked what is wrong with his current one he is categorical that the big issue is his girlfriend's inability to praise him. What he then realizes is that his need to be affirmed is paramount.

What you 'want' is therefore the opposite of what you don't want! Simple isn't it?

MAKE YOUR OWN LUCK

Some people are convinced that luck – good or bad – runs in families. How many of you come from a home where it was drummed into you that 'this family isn't lucky', 'good things never happen to us'? Stop and ask yourself if this is really true? If this family motto isn't one that was used in your family, then was there another type that is equally negative? Start to get more and more aware of what you say to yourself about change, possibilities of making change and whether you truly believe that something good can really happen to you. All of these things will greatly influence how much you 'hold on' and don't allow change.

FINDING YOUR NEEDS

Think again about the exercise on page 3, where you called to mind the thoughts and feelings you experience when you consider making a change in your life. Go back to that specific example for a moment. Put this book down and get a piece of paper or a diary or journal that you are going to use for these exercises.

First of all, bring that situation back into your mind. Take Sarah as an example. She is thinking of changing her job. She gets her piece of paper and writes near the top what it is she wants to change. We then ask her to write what has been happening to her that has led her to this decision. This is such a key thing. People so often trap themselves with asking the question 'Why do I want to do this?' It is as though you have put yourself on trial and you have to justify your desire for change. Well, stop right there. Instead, just think for a moment about your goal or wish. Write it down, but then think about what has been happening in the lead up to you formulating that wish or goal.

Take some time with that. If needs be, take a couple of days. If you don't explore what has been happening you will not be aware of what it is that you are likely to be holding on to later. It may also be that the more you think, the more negative thoughts and messages you will find about that lead up and this will help you move on, and move away from those negatives. Remember that it is more natural to want to move *away* from a negative than to try to persuade yourself to move *towards* one.

Sarah writes how she has worked in a firm of accountants as a senior secretary. She works very long hours and, at the age of 38, is beginning to resent the cost to her. This again is a key issue. Ask yourself, when you are ready, what does it cost you to continue doing whatever it is that you do (and that you are acknowledging that you want to change). Remember that you can do this with all areas of your life: work, personal, social, education, health etc. For Sarah, the costs are clear and far-reaching: she has no quality of family life. She has two children that are looked after by her mother. In the beginning, this worked for her, but she feels that she wants to see more of the children. She and her husband are very busy people. They don't earn a lot of money but live in London, which they find expensive so they don't feel that they have a lot of spare cash once the mortgage and bills are paid. They are both getting older and find that they are coping less well with the hours that they work and resent feeling exhausted at the weekends. The list continues to grow for Sarah the more she gets honest with herself.

Sarah's decision-making strategy then breaks down because she falls into the pit that most people fall into. She asks herself what is it she wants to do. Most times people falter at this question, or say

'I don't know what I want'. Well, if you are stuck, ask yourself different questions: 'What is it you need?', and 'What is it you need to do?'. Doesn't that feel different? This also helps you to stop holding on to what you always have done – because these questions help you acknowledge that you may simply not be doing whatever it is that you 'need'. You simply cannot move on while you are still holding on to 'wants' – especially when those wants don't work for you.

As we have said, you may not know what you 'want' to do but we are sure that you can more easily answer what it is that you don't want. Perhaps it isn't necessary to have a totally clear picture – perhaps things will become clearer as you move on. Again, remember that you don't have to have an absolutely precise plan at the outset – let that plan develop as you think things through.

Sarah also has to acknowledge that there is a danger for both her and her husband to 'hold' on to her salary as being a big reason why she cannot change. From this, the other areas that could be held on to emerge. Because of her salary they can afford to live in London – if they decide to move out of London and buy a cheaper house, Sarah can find a part-time job.

Think for a second about an old-fashioned set of scales, the ones that have two brass cups suspended from the arm of the scale by chains. The process of making a decision is mirrored by these scales. We go through one set of thoughts and load the scales in one direction and then we stop and begin to load the other side. This is called a 'decisional balance' and we can literally go back and forth many times in 'tipping the balance' one way and then the other. By focusing on the financial issue, Sarah has loaded the scales one way, but if she stops for a moment she can begin to tip them the other way. The issues that she would need to think about would be how much the quality of her life has been reduced because of the demands of her job.

Take some time to think about your needs. Don't block yourself with practical barriers; that again is something people do to trap themselves. We are not saying be reckless; what you are doing at the moment is some thinking and exploring – you are not going to put any of it into action until you are ready and it is all thought through. So each time you find a practical block, see if you can put it on one side. You need to concentrate on your needs – think about your goal or decision and really take stock of what has led you to think about it.

To help you further with the quest for clear wants and needs try this exercise:

Write a presentation of your life as you see it today. Be very precise and explicit. Write it as if you were going to teach someone to be you for a day. You, therefore, need to give background information and explanations for why you do things, and the ways that you do things.

Here is an example:

You are going to be Jo today. You are female, 41 years old. On weekdays, you get up at 5.30 am because you commute. You are very well organized. Your clothes will be laid out on a chair and your bag is packed with paperwork to look at on the train.

You always feel sad when leaving the house. You love it there but you also love your work and you need to work for a living...

You will obviously write a lot more than this, but the above should give you an idea of the detail required.

When you have written your presentation, go back through it and underline anything that stands out. There may be positives and negatives. There may be conflicts. There may be things that you have never seen so clearly.

As you think about change, don't be confused by how you respond emotionally. Change, whether it is perceived as for the good or not, is stressful. This is another reason why people often opt for keeping things the same: they often move from feeling excited to feeling stressed and they misinterpret that as a warning sign. Most people like to avoid stress, which is why they don't pursue change. So, remember, just because your stomach churns a bit it doesn't mean that it is a bad idea. Excitement and anxiety can actually feel very similar. So, whatever you do, don't confuse anxiety with excitement. Think about this and start to get more aware.

Stop for one moment and let's explore further how you may be blocking change and 'holding on':

1. TIME

How many times do you say:

When I have time I'd love to...
When I retire I'll take up...
I just don't have the time to think about this...
If I had time I would...

2. FEAR OR *F E A R* (*F*ALSE *E*VIDENCE *A*PPEARING *R*EAL)

The range of fear is infinitesimal. It can be fear of change, learning, making a mistake, fear of failure, fear of what people may think, their disapproval etc.

There can also be more subtle fears. If you make a big change in your life it is like stepping into the unknown. If you change career you are giving up a piece of your identity. People are also afraid of that very negative side of human beings – that if you change your status people may not want to know you. Issues of status, identity created by work, etc. are things that people will certainly want to hold on to. Who will you be if you stop being your occupation? For women and their identity, what does it really mean to have a baby?

3. ANXIETY

Remember that we are most often anxious because we are actually afraid that something won't happen. Or to put it another way, we desperately want something and we are afraid that it isn't going to happen. The next time you consider applying for a job and you feel anxious, just remind yourself not to confuse anxiety and excitement.

Also, think about why you may be anxious. If you really want that job, you are anxious that you are not going to get it. So turn that around into a positive, 'I really want this job', and you will immediately feel different. This helps you not to have to hold on to the anxiety and go down that destructive loop.

4. UNEXPLORED AND UNUSED POTENTIAL

People so often don't really know what their abilities are. You must not fall into the trap of telling yourself that you cannot do things if you don't actually know because you have never tried. There may also be things that you were useless at, at school for instance, which you may find are things that you can tackle in your adult life.

You may want to consider getting some expert help. If you want to explore making some changes in your work life then go to a careers consultant. Find out what your strengths and weaknesses are from someone who can objectively help you to answer those questions.

If you want to learn a new skill or subject then contact your local colleges or universities. Give yourself permission to have a go. You have nothing to lose by exploring, and everything to gain.

5. NOT EXERCISING CHOICE

Don't make life a series of brick walls with no windows of opportunity or doors to exit or enter from. Yes, you will have responsibilities – be they financial, personal, or both – but if you are not happy with your life, or you are feeling stuck or trapped, then something needs to change. To be realistic, you may not be able to make sweeping changes straightaway, but there will always be changes that can be made. So don't put obstacles in your way. Look at what can be changed and make that your starting point.

6. PERFECTIONISM

This takes up too much time and doesn't allow freedom to explore and make mistakes. No-one can be perfect all of the time. Don't set yourself up – you will never really enjoy anything until you let go of perfectionism.

7. CLUTTER AND OVERCOMPLICATIONS

One of the ways that people put obstacles in their way is by keeping life cluttered and overcomplicated.

Think about how we literally clutter our lives. What are we saying to ourselves psychologically when we hang on to things, put things in cupboards, the garage, the attic, etc. A great deal has been said about Feng Shui, the Eastern art of ordering your surroundings to improve all aspects of your life. Well, there are simple lessons to be learned from it. It is easy to get bogged down when you are wading through things that belong to the past and really have no future use. Start to look around your home and get ruthless. You don't have to throw things away – give them to people who will really benefit. Then feel the difference.

Emotionally, you have to do the same thing. Are you cluttered by your past? Be really honest with yourself. So often people don't want to look back at difficult areas. They prefer to cover them up and try to forget them rather than face them and do something about them.

Think about these questions:

1 How much do you talk on and on about an unresolved problem, conflict or incident? It may be a broken relationship, a problem at work that has never been sorted out, and argument with a friend that still haunts you – the list is endless.
2 Are you wary of people who remind you of someone who hurt you? Do you judge them and fear them rather than finding out what they are like?
3 Do you hold on to memories in the fear that, if you forget, 'it' will happen again?

SUMMARY

- Start to think about the anchors that keep you stuck because they make you feel safe, either because they are familiar to you or because they actually create some sense of safety. We are not suggesting you become reckless but that you learn to recognize the elements that stop you moving on. Start to believe that you can do something about them, and that nothing bad needs to happen.

- Change does not have to be 100 per cent. You can allow yourself to make gradual and small changes. In this way, you avoid the fear of having to let go of some anchors that feel really important to you.

- Anchors have many guises. Keep aware of them as you continue to learn to recognize them.

- Do not be ruled by **F E A R** – false evidence appearing real. It is a powerfully negative tool that keeps you firmly anchored in being unable to change.

- Don't confuse anxiety with excitement. The feelings are very similar. You will feel more motivated if you remind yourself how excited you are, as well as understanding that anxiety is normal but is not a sign of impending disaster!

- Watch out for your own internal dialogue as well as what happens when you consider change. Do you visualize change, for example, or experience it in some other way? Awareness of this will help you to stay motivated when you tackle any task or change. You can call on the strategies that help you feel more motivated.

CHAPTER 2

Lost Property

This chapter looks at your past and what you may be carrying from it that is getting in your way today. You may also have developed the habit of taking on board other people's problems and difficulties which leave you depleted and exhausted. You need to generate a greater awareness and learn to start to 'let go' of the past and concentrate on being free enough to make the most of today. By being less cluttered you will also have the energy to contemplate change and not be ruled by messages that really no longer apply – or may never have applied! This chapter contains a number of exercises that will help you generate a more powerful state of awareness, as well as some assignments at the end that will help you start to 'let go'.

FACING YOUR PAST

There will be many reasons why you get held back from making changes, and the chances are that it is you who does the holding back. To understand this properly, you need to be prepared to face your past, and what you carry from it emotionally and psychologically. You need to really explore the journey you have made so far and not be afraid of it – keeping it locked up is not the way to move forward. Don't have skeletons in your cupboard – get them out in the privacy of your mind – by doing so they lose power. Neither should you tell yourself that it 'doesn't matter', or that 'much worse things happen to other people'. Your experiences should not be devalued by comparing them to others'. So by looking at your past and facing it you will gain strength, insight and understanding – believe us. You will also gain energy by not having to carry certain things around with you any more. People often say to us 'what's the point? Nothing can be changed'. Yes, that's right, the past cannot be changed, but you can change today and the negative effects yesterday may be having. Favourite expressions that people use are 'I've put a layer of concrete on it', 'I just pretend it didn't happen'. The question you need to ask yourself is, does any of that really sound healthy to you?

WAYS YOU COPE

While you explore your childhood and the past, it is also helpful to look at ways you have found to cope with life and all that it has thrown at you. Quite often, children and teenagers use methods of coping that can actually backfire in adult life. Take avoidance as one example – children find exams stressful, so they avoid study to help alleviate the stress. Obviously, this doesn't really work. Many adults reflect on how one layer of avoidance fuelled several others until it became a destructive way of life. If this is the case, this needs to be faced and dealt with. Avoidance systematically destroys your confidence so it will have to be rebuilt bit by bit. Another example of a negative coping strategy is the 'layer of concrete' – all that you basically create is a public face that may seem confident and impenetrable but underneath there will be this totally different person who needs to be taken care of in a very different way. While you are thinking about this, ask yourself, 'who benefits?'. You can't. So who are you doing it for? Remember, too, that vulnerability is not weakness; it is a very special part of being human. If you don't allow yourself to be vulnerable you will never have a truly intimate relationship with anyone.

DON'T BE AFRAID TO EXPLORE

If you are considering moving quickly on to the next chapter, just hold on for a second. You shouldn't jump to any quick conclusion that this chapter isn't for you, or run from what we are saying. You may feel that there were no 'problems' as you were growing up. We are not asking you to look for something that wasn't there, or to label your childhood as problematic if it wasn't. Everyone will benefit by doing this exploration – there may not have been 'problems' as such in your early days, but there may be things that do need looking at. Consider issues such as your confidence, how you view taking risks, your self-esteem, self-image, ability to cope healthily with life – if any of these things feel lacking, then the root of this needs to be traced. Ask yourself 'what happened?' or 'didn't happen?' that made you feel like this. However you are at the moment, start to think about what it would be like to feel better about yourself, to feel more confident, to have the self-belief to try things and take reasonable risks.

WHAT REALLY BELONGS TO YOU?

The first thing we want you to start thinking about is what you are carrying that doesn't belong to you. If that doesn't immediately make sense to you, think of a lost property office that is filled with other people's things. There may be an item that has been there for such a long time that no one can remember when it was put in. As for the original owner, they may have never claimed it. And why not? Because they probably no longer have any use for it. They have probably even forgotten they had it in the first place. Key people in our lives do exactly the same thing. They literally hand us things and we land up storing them. Let's give you some clear examples to think about.

On one level, there will probably be many examples from your place of work or home life. If you hold a fairly senior position, you will be used to people coming to you with their work problems. Do you find in the work place that you get exhausted and distracted by other people's problems and lose vital time and energy for your own? Do you end up doing too much for others and taking on their worries and work as well as yours?

Similar things can happen in your personal relationships. Do you find that you shoulder responsibilities for others, and end up running their lives as well as yours? If you are married, or in a relationship, are you always the one to make decisions and make things happen? Are you too much in charge of other people's lives, other people who happen to be capable adults?

There will also be examples from other levels in your personal life. How these are experienced will be extremely varied but just read these few illustrations and see what comes up for you. These examples are about the impact of roles and parental expectations.

YOUR DREAMS OR SOMEONE ELSE'S?

Many people make career and relationship choices influenced by the wishes of their parents. It may be that they are realizing a dream for their parents or simply continuing the family tradition. The problem comes if this choice really does not suit you. What you may end up with is simply someone else's 'lost property' – your motivation to do what you are doing didn't really come from you; it was about someone else and their wishes and aspirations. Stop for a second and think about the effect of expectations in your life. If you are not happy with some of the choices you have made, give yourself permission to re-examine them. You are allowed more than one choice and you are also allowed to change your mind.

WHOSE RESPONSIBILITY?

It is also important to look at the role that you had in your family, especially if there were any kind of problems between your parents. Did you, for example, have to support your parents emotionally in any way, or did you have to look after your siblings because Mum or Dad couldn't? Without you really knowing why, were you elevated by default to a position or set of responsibilities that really belonged to someone else? This can be for many reasons, such as ill-health, alcoholism, mental illness, lack of their own role models. The reasons may be irrelevant but the effects are not.

NO TALK RULE

Lost property gains a power of its own because, when you carry other people's 'stuff', it tends not to be talked about. At the time of taking it on, if it were in childhood, there would probably have been a 'no talk rule'. Again, let us give you an example of this by using the experiences of someone brought up in a alcoholic family. Dad drinks too much and Mum has difficulty coping. Jack is the oldest child and tries to help Mum and look after her emotionally. Jill is younger and grows up resenting how close Jack and Mum are. Jack grows up mourning the loss of his childhood and bewildered as to what was the matter with Dad. Mum didn't tell Jack because she didn't want him to be upset. Jack has struggled with the effects of seeing the terrible rows that his parents had and has subsequently feared any intimate relationship as a result. When he started talking to Mum and found out the missing pieces, he realized that his fear was about someone else's experiences and not his own. This set him free of potentially damaging lost property. What's more, Jack has learned that the world is a less frightening place if people talk to each other and be honest. Jack had spent his life filling in the blanks and guessing rather than finding security by asking questions and at least getting part of the truth.

Put the book down for a second and think about what you store for other people. Write down some thoughts.

MAKE AN INVENTORY

So as you make your journey through life you are obviously exposed to people, places, other people's emotions and problems, and they all leave their mark. Some are, of course, positive; others are not.

What we need to do is make a thorough inventory. From doing that you can decide what needs to go – what really doesn't belong to you. It may be that you are going to confront extremely painful areas in your life. If you do, then write only what is SAFE AND COMFORTABLE.

To do the inventory you need to be as thorough as you can but you don't necessarily have to write huge amounts (you can if you want to). People often find writing things down helps them really concentrate and think about things in depth. To make the inventory you need to do the following. Think about each section and respond by answering the questions: 'What is it that needs to be understood? What are the key points?'

- Try to describe your family life and childhood. Don't get blocked by trying to describe it as either positive or negative, just try to describe it as it was. Remember that inventories consist of positives and negatives, but at this particular point we will be focusing on areas that may be causing you difficulty today.
- Move on and think about your school life. How did you get on at school? What sort of relationships did you have with your classmates and teachers? Were school days a time that you look back at with happiness or sadness or a mixture of both?
- Move on and focus on your teen years and critical milestones that you remember. At this time you will have started to be aware of your own sexuality. What memories do you have of this time? What do you feel when you recollect those times? Did you or do you have any confusions or difficulties related to this?
- Move on again and focus on your later teen years. Did you continue in higher education, or did you start to work? Does anything stand out from this time that you may need to look at?
- Think about your personal relationships in general. What again stands out as you look back over your life? Are there any patterns or concerns?

KEY TO THE NEXT EXERCISE

Now that you have done this inventory we want you to start to increase your awareness of a few key things. This next exercise is about gaining awareness in a slightly different way. It is about you starting to feel liberated, about how to avoid certain blocks to feeling good and enjoying life. This exercise will also help you continue to recognize more 'lost property' as well as begin to be more in contact with what really belongs to you and who and what you are.

Lesson number one is to realize that the real you is the spiritual you – the life force within you (the concept of spirituality will be dealt with in greater depth in Chapter 13). This is the part of you that enables you to feel wonderful and happy. That is, of course, if you are able to be in contact with it. It is more than likely, though, that you will mistakenly believe that the real you is something to do with the role you play, the way you feel, your personality, your appearance, your past experiences. This is not strictly true – these are simply labels, and experiences.

If you don't believe us, just stop and watch a baby or toddler for 10 minutes – notice the joy of life that they have. From your own experiences, you will know if something is getting in the way of you enjoying life, taking up challenges and giving yourself permission to do things differently. More often than not it will manifest itself as some sort of negative voice or the 'negative' side of you. You may even have a name for it or a description of it. We have heard some people call it 'the little man on my shoulder'. We have always rather liked this concept. It conjures up all sorts of pictures and images.

This negative voice, or its embodiment, only serves one purpose, and that is negativity and unhappiness. It has no sense of balance or fairness; it just thrives on making you feel bad. This negative voice convinces you that reliving bad past experiences is good; worrying about the future is good; analysing everything is good; holding yourself back is good; and carrying lots of lost property is good.

If this sounds completely daft to you, just hang on. We are sure that you are aware of a negative voice inside you. We all have them but you may not be so aware of yours yet.

So put the book down and think back to times in your life when you have really wanted to do something. Try and transport yourself back to that specific time and think about how you felt and what you were thinking. Try to remember what sort of 'internal dialogue' happened.

Take Peter, for example. He really wanted to go to night classes to improve some of his computer skills. He was beginning to feel embarrassed at work because so many younger staff were computer literate. He told us that he had sent off for a prospectus and had filled out an application form. Then his negative voice started: 'Why bother? You are so behind these other people, you'll never catch up. I bet other people on this course will be much younger and you will just look a fool. You don't have time – you'll start this and then regret ever committing yourself'. See what we mean? By the time Peter had listened to all of this he had nearly been talked out of doing it. Luckily, he didn't, and it worked out quite differently to what the negative inner voice had been suggesting.

Can you identify with any of these phrases? Can you also think of others? Just remember that the negative voice has only one tone – so it is reasonably easy to spot once you have improved your awareness.

So, lesson number one is to increase your awareness. If you are aware, then become more aware. Awareness is the antidote to a lot of negatives.

The next thing we want you to do is to think about the negative voice. What do you picture when you think about it? Do you actually see 'a little man on your shoulder' or something else? If you do, try to describe him/her/it? Whatever you do, don't put the book down. Stop for a second and think about this. If you hear this negative voice, can you actually go one stage further and start describing it? Some of you may even be able to picture it. If you can do this then attempt to draw it. If not, a brief description will do. Whatever you do, don't let the voice tell you not to do this exercise!

The next step is to write down some of the things that this negative voice says. You should be able to add to this list each time you catch yourself listening to this voice. In the meantime, think about those negative messages we all have, such as 'good luck doesn't run in this family', or whatever. Where did that message come from? Is it really true? Even more important, does it really help you in your day-to-day life? If you answer no to all these questions, then 'chuck it out'. How do you do that? By confronting that message whenever it appears. Keep challenging it. Keep checking with yourself as to its validity and relevance. Sometimes we do things because they have become a habit, and we need to know that we can stop at any time.

WHY DO YOU CARRY LOST PROPERTY?

You need to remember that children are like blotting paper. As you were growing up you will have absorbed everything that went on around you. Unfortunately, however, children also tend to feel responsible for all that happens around them. As a result, they will sometimes carry the effects of other people's negative actions. These can be abuse – sexual, mental or physical; rows between parents which may involve violence; affects of parents' marital breakdown, etc. The important point is that people carry the effects of others' behaviour towards them or towards those whom they love. Sometimes you need to do a check to see if you are still carrying these effects with you.

You may also carry lost property because human beings need to feel in control, and they tell themselves that they are in control. Therefore, if something bad happens, like an assault, burglary, rape, car accident, etc., one of the ways that people cope with this psychologically is to tell themselves that it was really their fault. So what human beings need to do to cope actually backfires upon them. For instance, we can imagine the effect of a woman blaming herself for being raped. Letting go of lost property is about letting ourselves off the hook, and taking the blame off ourselves. Life 'happens', and sometimes we have no control.

So as you come to the end of this chapter, we want you to ask yourselves if you are carrying hurt, anger, shame or guilt to yourself or someone or several people in your life. If you are, you need to consider writing a 'therapeutic letter'. This is a letter written for your own benefit. *It is not meant to be sent.* Write as many letters as you need, and take your time. Write as if you were speaking to the person concerned and really say (no holds barred) what you need to say. Remember, also, that this is a private matter and the letter should not be seen by anyone else, so keep it in a safe place, or burn it when you are finished.

You may also want to write a letter to yourself. To help you do this, you need first to imagine some real person that you truly love being in your position. How would you treat that person, what would you say? You then need to show such kindness and support to yourself. No matter how much you resist it, this is something you must consider doing. Again, take your time.

You also need to think about how other people's life views affect you. There are some people who are genuinely very negative. DON'T TRY TO CHANGE THEM. But think about shielding yourself. Ensure that you have people in your life who can give you some positives.

Think also about negative influences from people that genuinely did not intend to hurt or damage you. It may be that we have lost a loved one, or someone has become very ill physically or mentally. These negative influences can be very difficult to deal with because people feel guilty at feeling anger. Later on in the book there will be exercises to help you look at these situations from a different angle.

SUMMARY

A key theme of this chapter is raising your awareness and in turn gaining a valuable insight that will help you move on. So from now on you need to be more aware of lost property and its effects.

- Do you take on board other people's problems?

  ____

- Can you start to 'let go' of the past?

  ____

- Is it really you who is holding yourself back with negative coping styles, such as a layer of concrete avoidance?

  ____

- Become aware of what you carry for others:
  Taking too much responsibility
  Realizing others' expectations for them
  Trying to solve problems that aren't yours to solve.

  ____

- Get free by talking about things. You will then possibly gain information or clarity and stop filling in blanks.

- The inventory helps you to get clearer and pinpoint areas that need your attention. You may see patterns emerging. All of this will leave you with the energy and resources to move forwards.

- The 'negative voice' exercise pulls the themes of the chapter together and again pushes towards greater awareness.

- You are not your role in life.

- Your negative voice is no friend. It does not tell you the truth. It prevents change by taking away your power.

- If you are feeling angry, write a letter.

CHAPTER 3

Who Gives to the Giver?

This chapter asks you to look at how much time you give to others and what really motivates you to do it. In exploring these issues you need to consider the many different areas in your life, beginning with your family, current partner and children (if you have them). For those of you in employment, it will clearly also extend to your work colleagues and clients. Finally, there will also be the time that you give to your friends and more distant relatives. If you were to count them up, there would be quite a number of people who make demands upon your time.

Take a typical week and think about the following:

- How much time do you give to doing things for others?
- How much time do you spend thinking about others, worrying about them, discussing them? Be as specific as you can.
- Have there been things in the last week you have not done for yourself because you've been left with no time?

- Do you see other consequences of giving too much to others – are there specific examples?
- Can you see examples in the last week of you having created expectations that made it very difficult to say no?

Some of the time spent on others will fall into your natural 'duties' and 'obligations' but some may go well beyond that. Do you tend, for example, to focus too much on other people because you can't give to yourself? Or are there people in your life who make huge demands because they are physically or mentally ill or suffer with problems like alcoholism, drug addiction or eating disorders? You may, therefore, not be willingly giving your time but simply feel that you are literally being held to ransom. Or do you just feel completely drained by your family responsibilities and afraid to admit you are just not coping because it is expected that you should (or so you feel)?

There are lots of people who tend to do more for others than themselves. We are not saying that there isn't a good and healthy side to doing things for others. You need, however, to ask yourself whether doing as much as you do is doing you any good? Does it also become one of the major reasons why you never do anything for yourself and thus never open yourself up to change, or have the energy required for changing? Have you lost a sense of 'you' because of your day-to-day obligations.

This 'giving' or 'caring' can fall into several different categories, which we will now look at in some detail.

THE DEFLECTORS

Some people deliberately focus on others to avoid confronting themselves – but this is often heavily disguised! Think about a few of these scenarios. Are you drawn to people who have the same problems as you? Do you go to the ends of the earth to sort these people out but do nothing for yourself? Or are you more of a 'wounded carer', throwing yourself into charity or voluntary work because you feel so bad about yourself – or do you do it for healthy reasons? Or are you 'the hero'? How many times in the last few months have you told people that you are 'fine' when you have been feeling terrible, telling yourself that others have their own problems and you cannot burden them with yours?

If you feel your hackles rise as you read this, don't worry – we are not going to start throwing any labels at you. We just want you to take a deep breath and think about this because it is going to be a big stumbling block if you don't get honest about it.

Put the book down for a second. Get honest with yourself – what does this do to you? What does it cost you to walk around being 'caring' to everyone but yourself? What does it do to hide behind a mask? What does it do to act as if you are perfectly OK when you are really crumbling inside? What does it do to tell yourself that no one is that interested in you or only cares for you because you are 'problem free'.

If you don't identify with any of this, it is nevertheless wise to think about it and watch out for it. Sometimes people have difficulty really seeing themselves, and this again becomes one of the major reasons why they can't move on. If you haven't really given yourself an opportunity to get to know yourself, you will never be aware of the pluses and minuses, or the blocks and hurdles, that you may need to get over or around.

To get you really thinking about this, do the following exercise:

1) Cut out a mask from a piece of paper. Don't worry about what it looks like. Just leave two spaces for your eyes.
2) On the outer side, write down as many things as you can about what people see when they look at you. So it may be a physical description. Also, what do you want people to see? What do people know about you?
3) On the other side, write down what you don't show to others or what you try hard to conceal about yourself.
4) Compare the two sides. How different are they? What are the penalties of trying to pretend that you are something you are not? What are the penalties of hiding the real you?

BEING ASSERTIVE

What about being assertive – getting your needs met in a non-aggressive way? If you are locked into caretaking everyone else's feelings (because this is exactly what 'carers' do), it is easy to get locked into not saying anything about what you want and need. This can quite often become some sort of emotional volcano that simply waits to blow. No human being can survive simply by running around after other people and putting everyone else first. What 'drives' human beings is getting their needs met (not to be confused with wants). We have basic needs for food, water and shelter but we also need to love and be loved. This basic human need manifests itself in all sorts of different ways and radiates through our lives, taking many different paths and courses.

Put the book down again for a second and think about your needs. Here is an example of Sarah's needs:

- I need companionship from my partner and to feel loved and respected.
- I need to feel that I am important to those whom I love.
- I need people around me.
- I need support.
- I need rest.
- I need to laugh.
- I need food, shelter and warmth.
- I need a holiday!

Use this only as a guide and try to list as many needs as you can. When you have done this, put big red circles around any that are not being currently attended to. Ask yourself why not. Have you fallen into the trap of getting needs met from external sources and 'things', such as status and work. Have these 'needs' overtaken the more fundamental ones?

Here is a step-by-step guide to getting your needs met:

1 Identify the need and be honest with yourself about it.
2 Squash the 'counter-arguments' from your negative inner voice. Needs are needs – they are not right or wrong, weak or self-indulgent.
3 Start letting significant people know that you have these needs – people closest to you are not mind-readers!

Have you ever seen the 'Bill of Rights'? No, this is nothing to do with the United States! It is a therapeutic bill of rights. We want you to look at this list and tick off as many rights as you are aware are being met.

Bill of Rights

Everyone has the right to:

- Be treated respectfully.
- Be listened to.
- Ask for what they need.
- Have their feelings listened to.
- Change their mind.
- Make mistakes.
- Choose to 'let things go...'
- To say 'no'.

Not many people would tick all of them, but if you are scoring too low then stop and think. You have rights and needs and you have a right for them to be met. It does not mean that it has to be at someone else's cost. Think about that for a moment. If you are projecting your own experiences on to others – you give a lot to others and you feel that this leaves you with no time and a lot of hidden resentment – then it would be natural for you to fear that this is how other people would experience fulfilling some of your needs. But when people are looking after themselves, giving to others does not need to be a costly exercise. From now on, remember not to project your feelings on to others. Or to put it more simply, don't imagine that everyone feels the way that you do.

Think about the messages you give, or don't give, to people about your needs. Do you ever really let people know what you need? You may wish that someone would be able to guess but that is beside the point. You need to accept that people are not the mind-readers we would like them to be. Often even those closest to us take us at 'face value'. Make a decision today that you will work on the needs you have circled in red. If, for example, you are feeling the need for support, then start asking for it. If that negative voice of yours is telling you that it is weak to ask for support or that you shouldn't need it, then stop for a moment. This voice is wrong. Needs are needs – it is as simple and straightforward as that. It is as ridiculous as saying that we shouldn't need to drink water – we do, and we would obviously die without it. Well, our emotional needs are as life-threatening if they are not met. Okay, you won't die, but you do die inside. If your needs aren't being met you will know exactly what we mean.

Start gradually and don't jump in at the deep end. When you begin to let people know about your needs, you may find that you feel vulnerable and possibly also very angry. If you have been leading your life disregarding your needs and desperately hoping that someone will mind-read, then all those years of stored feelings, resentments and disappointments will surface.

FAMILY RESPONSIBILITIES

Many women with family responsibilities tend to put their partner and children first all of the time rather than giving themselves permission to sometimes be first. A lot of women say that they feel like their lives are 'on hold', waiting for the day that they will have some time to think about themselves. Obviously, some of this is completely 'natural', but when it is taken to an extreme it is damaging. The key questions to ask yourself are:

- Are you doing this to the detriment of yourself?
- Are you feeling resentful and angry? (You may not be directly voicing it but is this happening?)

Lone Parents

It is also very important to address one-parent families. You may be a lone mother or father bringing up children. This may be through divorce, separation, bereavement or occasionally through choice. Many people rally around a lone father because he will tend to be seen as having to undertake an unfamiliar role, whereas many single women are expected to cope. As for those who choose to be a 'single' parent, there are perhaps again unfair expectations that preclude you from asking for help.

For any lone parent there is the danger of becoming isolated. The lone mother may be excluded from social events that will be attended by couples. Lone fathers often say that they are treated with a degree of suspicion because they are performing a traditionally female role. How many lone fathers would be invited round to a get-together of young mums?

The Breadwinner

Some men feel that they have total responsibility for providing for the family, and let that pressure mount. This can lead to ill health, resentment, feelings of anger, etc. Men have feelings and vulnerabilities, but often don't feel that they can speak about them. In today's economic climate, a lot of men can no longer be the 'breadwinner' or single breadwinner. There are also constant fears of redundancy, and some men will feel that they cannot talk to their partners about this. They feel 'less than inadequate'. Carrying all of this can lead to huge feelings of resentment.

CARING PROFESSIONALS

Some people who work in the caring professions let their work spill into their private lives. What is it like to be a professional carer, particularly for younger people who enter these professions? What sort of stresses and strains are they under and whom can they go to when they are having problems? Consider a young doctor who finds the death of a patient difficult and upsetting – many would be afraid to show that they are in difficulties. Also, think about counsellors, nurses, therapists, social workers, teachers, police – the list is probably quite endless. If you are in any type of a 'caring' profession, who takes care of you? What do you do to off-load your problems? What do you do if you are really concerned about someone in your care?

NON-PROFESSIONAL CARERS

Some people are full-time carers for a sick relative or friend. The word 'sick' covers many problem areas, such as alcoholism, eating disorders, mental illnesses, physical and mental disability, terminal illness. How many of you are suffering almost in silence? When was the last time a friend or member of your family sat you down and asked you how you really are? How tired are you? How scared are you? As we said in the Introduction, there are areas that we would dream of changing in our lives and they are not going to change unless there is a miracle. Those of you who are nursing terminally ill loved ones, or physically and mentally handicapped people, know that the problem is not going to change or go away, but we would hope that you are going to examine what you can do differently to look after yourself. The same goes for someone who is coping with a loved one with an addiction problem. Yes, there may be hope of change for that person, but you need as the 'carer' to be concentrating more on you and taking care of yourself. We all need to be aware of working on changing what really can be changed and not focusing and blocking ourselves by what cannot or will not be changed.

We know that a lot of you will hear this last paragraph as 'more work'. We know from people we have worked with that there are natural wishes such as 'why can't someone just run around after me for a change?', 'why can't I have just one day off?', 'why can't people see what I'm going through?' etc. Why does it have to be me to instigate things changing? Well, this will never happen unless you start asking for help for yourself and letting people know how you really are. People who really need help are often seen by those closest to them as 'copers'. Yes, this is true – you probably are a coper, but that does not make you superhuman. Why not start to let people know how you really are rather than coming across as someone without any needs? In this way, people may start to realize what you are really going through and offer to help you in some small way. So remember that looking after yourself is greatly about you starting to get honest about how you feel and being able to 'drop that mask'.

MAKING CHANGES

The question we have is: what do you miss out on when you don't focus on yourself? What are the negatives of doing this, and what is it that you miss out on achieving? How does it really feel not to put yourself in a position to receive affirmation, kindness, time, help, comfort from other people? We bet there are a lot of you that secretly desire all of these things but you simply don't actively go out and seek them or make it apparent that this is what is needed. What does that say about how you feel about yourself? What does that do to the relationships you have with those closest to you. How angry and resentful do you end up feeling?

Where does this resentment go? Most of the time it will come out sideways. Often, when people get really honest with their friends and families, people will begin to admit that there has been a lot of anger.

If you really want to take a risk, you may want to stop and consider 'how does my family see me?'. You may then want to ask some members to answer this question for you, if you feel comfortable to do so.

If you are truly needed by other people – be it as a mother, father, carer, professional carer, brother, sister, friend, or whatever – your wellbeing is paramount. What would actually happen if you couldn't cope? What would happen if you became too ill to go on? We are not asking these questions to scare you but to get you thinking. You can't drive yourself into the ground emotionally or physically – it just simply won't work. You need to start somewhere and soon.

What about starting from now with a promise to begin to look after yourself? We're not suggesting anything major. What small thing can you commit, solely for yourself, to doing today? We know you can't see us but we just ducked to avoid the barrage of reasons why this can't happen. Stop that now. You have to make a start, no matter how small. Even if it is that you take just five minutes for yourself – do it and do it today. You could consider:

- Taking time to talk to someone, such as a friend or your partner.
- Giving yourself a treat, like a bubble bath, reading a magazine or just shutting your eyes.

We hope that this chapter will have helped you identify the degree to which you are a giver and or carer. We are acknowledging that some of you have been elected to this role because of circumstances and not through choice. Others of you have chosen your role. The thing is that it doesn't entirely matter. The most important thing is that you appreciate why changes need to be made and that you start to see a life for yourself, no matter how much the odds are stacked against you.

From now on, you need to get really honest with yourself as to what the pitfalls are for you, as well as getting you to count the cost (emotionally, spiritually, physically, mentally, socially and financially). If you are, for example, extremely resentful, then the cost is too high. Resentment does nothing but breed further negatives and is not good for your health. The cost may also be far more subtle – you may simply be giving far too much time and energy to others and not leading any part of your life for yourself. Deep down inside there may be an extreme sadness that you simply do not have time for yourself, or simply cannot give time to yourself. From now on you need to start treating yourself like a thing of value. However well you treat others, some of that time, energy and care needs to be directed to you. Believe us: you will feel better about yourself if you start doing that right now.

Sit down now and do this exercise. Make sure that you will not be disturbed so find somewhere private and quiet. Shut your eyes and cast your mind right back to when you day-dreamed about your adulthood. Can you remember some specific times from your childhood or teen years when you thought about being an adult and what you wanted to achieve? What picture you had of what you would be like? What did you want to have in your life? What did that picture look like? Did you once have hobbies and interests that you thoroughly enjoyed that you have simply dropped? Hobbies and pastimes are so important. They are experiences that you can lose yourself in, express yourself in and simply enjoy. If you have dropped all your hobbies, then make a pledge now to take one of them up – one of them must be possible. The possibilities are endless. We have known people take up sports years after stopping, going back to playing an instrument, taking singing lessons, stamp collecting, reading, painting…

We also need to ask you one further important question. Who do you go to when you are in trouble and need to talk? Be honest. Do you have a couple of friends you can talk to? Do you talk to your partner? Do you feel comfortable with asking for help?

If something is really worrying you, do you tend more to keep it to yourself? Are you afraid of burdening other people, or looking as if you cannot cope? Are you afraid of showing that sometimes you do not have the answers? This is such a key issue when it comes to making changes – you can't always have the answers so you need to tap into resources around you to find them.

If you have identified with this chapter in any way, one thing is very clear: you need some support, and somewhere and some time to off-load. It doesn't have to be a huge amount of time. This is so often how people block themselves – that good old 'I haven't got time'. Make time, and also think about how much you tell others about day-to-day problems that you may be facing. You might not want to divulge all – that is normal – but what about making a start by off-loading some of it and see whether that leads you to go further? If you don't do it you will never realize that it really is not as scary as you might think. If you take risks with those who are close to you, you will find that your relationships deepen, and if you are caught up in that 'giving' spiral, you need that connection and you need to feel it as strongly as possible.

SUMMARY

- Be specific and clear about how much time and energy you give to others.

- Is it healthy giving or are you avoiding yourself and your problems, or trying to bolster a flagging self-esteem?

- Be honest about your motives because this may well be a big block to change.

- Start to understand your needs and give them attention. Needs are not self-indulgent, they are as essential as a supply of water and food. Let significant people know your needs – they are not mind-readers.

- Try to find more of a balance with your responsibilities – there may be occasions when you can ask for help but you are not doing so. Be aware of the risks of not having help, such as a build up of anger and resentment.

- There may be situations in which any change seems impossible, but look again.

- Believe that you deserve support and co-operation.

CHAPTER 4

Too Many Passengers

The people in your life can be thought of as 'passengers'. It is not always the number of passengers that creates the problem. The key question is more about how you handle your own particular set of passengers and, of course, what they are like.

You do, however, have a choice. You can obsess about those passengers you feel make life difficult for you, or you can decide this minute that something is going to change, and that change has to happen inside you. In other words, stop trying to 'control the uncontrollable' and focus your energies on yourself. Too many people make the great mistake of spending years wishing that other people would change – and guess what? It doesn't usually happen. The one person you can change is yourself, and if you make changes and do things differently you may just find that your relationships will improve, that your changes will have a knock-on effect. As you work on changing your behaviour, you also need to concentrate on taking responsibility. Look at the contribution you have made to some of your difficulties with problem passengers by actually 'teaching them' that it is alright to behave badly, not take responsibility, not to give you any support, and not to work as a team with you.

There is also bound to be a tug of war between time, your responsibilities, your need for fulfilment and achievement, and the key people in your life. This can lead to you feeling that there is simply too little time for you and too many people making demands on it. This can often lead to huge feelings of guilt and resentment and sets up a vicious circle. This is not the basis for a good relationship, and everyone will suffer until you decide to do something differently. If your relationships are causing you unhappiness and guilt, you need to do something. Stop accepting that your relationships have to be like this. They don't. If you don't do something, the guilt will lead to resentment and anger and back and forth until you end up resenting those who are the most precious to you, and feeling that whatever you do you will not be able to satisfy everyone, let alone yourself. Imagine for one second what it would be like not to have to spend so much time feeling annoyed, angry, ashamed, defeated, hurt and isolated by some of your passengers. The key lies with you – but we don't mean that we expect you to take all the responsibility. There is a difference between taking responsibility in a healthy way and taking control and respon-sibility for everything.

Your passenger list can include very personal relationships through to casual acquaintances, and in total there will be quite a number of people on the list:

1 The family you were born into. This will include your parents, siblings, aunts and uncles, etc.
2 The family that you go on to create – your partner and children.
3 The family you become a part of when you form a long-term relationship with someone. This may include children from a previous relationship, in-laws, etc.
4 Your work colleagues, staff that you supervise or employ.
5 Friends and acquaintances.

6 Those who pass very briefly through your life. These may be people that are employed for a brief period (such as builders, decorators, etc.) and short-term acquaintances.

To deal more effectively with your passengers, you need to start by taking some time to think about your own set of expectations and rules. Break your relationships down into different categories (life partner, current partner, parents, etc.) and think about what your expectations are of that particular relationship.

First, think about your current partner and put the book down. Take a breath and start by being honest:

1 What do you expect? Have your expectations changed over time?
2 What are the 'rules' of the relationship as far as you are concerned:
   Do you want an equal partnership, or something different?
   What are your thoughts on roles? Are they well defined?
   What about fidelity?
   What about time for hobbies, personal time?
   What are your thoughts on children and child care?
   What about your physical relationship?
3 How much does your partner know about how you think and feel? Do you make an effort to find out how they are, what they are currently thinking and feeling? We want you to think really hard about this point, and keep thinking about it. You have to be prepared to let your partner know more about you and for you to take the time to ask about them. Yes, it can make you very vulnerable, but it could also create a relationship that will bring you great happiness.

At the end of the chapter you will get to see lists of expectations from different couples – this will show you just how varied expectations can be.

When you are ready, think about what expectations you have in other relationships and what the rules are. Again, ask yourself whether you ever let these people know what you expect, want and need. Remember that to feel contentment you have to work towards your expectations and reality meeting – the greater the gap the less satisfied and happy you will be.

Now we want you to look at some key points for building better relationships. You will see that the foundation lies initially in being prepared to communicate and listen.

---

1 Don't expect those closest to you to be mind-readers. It would be nice if we didn't have to ask for help. In other words, if people close to us would notice when we were in difficulties or upset and spontaneously ask. But that is not reality. If you have a problem, if you are upset, if you need help, then SPEAK.
2 If you and your partner (or friend, etc.) need to talk about a problem:
Listen to what is being said.
Don't interrupt each other.
No raised voices, insults or threats.
Don't attempt to discuss who is right and who is wrong. Why not talk about how you feel instead? Feelings are not right or wrong. If someone is hurt then acknowledge it. Don't 'fight to the death' to prove who is in the wrong. People feel better if they feel they have been listened to. You can demonstrate this back to them by saying 'I understand that you are really upset', etc.

Don't feel obliged to agree. You can agree to differ. It really is not the end of the world.
Don't jump to find a 'solution'. Work towards compromises over issues like time management, taking time for yourself, child-care arrangements.

3 If there is a crisis:
Isolate it. Relationships go through problems, but a crisis does not have to contaminate the whole of your relationship. Remember to speak about what is good in the relationship.
Utilize the time you have been together and the knowledge you have of each other. Don't suddenly become strangers.
To overcome the problem, there has to be an agreement that you will work together to resolve it.
Don't be afraid to ask for professional help. It is extremely difficult to be objective if you are hurt and angry.

Not only do you need to be aware of your own expectations, but those of others as well. Throughout your life you will be in many different relationships with people who have their own expectations and agendas, probably leaving you feeling at times like there are just too many passengers with perhaps too many different demands, expectations, wants and needs. Relationships may become a major juggling act that can leave you exhausted and frustrated. Alternatively, you can stop doing all the work and leave some room for co-operation. The choice is yours – work so hard that you become some sort of exhausted hero, or let others do their share of the work. In these situations, people will often say things like 'Oh, I thought you didn't want to help' or 'But you are such a coper' or 'I feel a failure around you because you always do so much'.

GAMES PEOPLE PLAY

Another big change that you can commit to is to stop engaging in other people's games.

Tug of War

Problems arise when people cannot or will not co-operate, leaving you to take a huge amount of responsibility. When you are experiencing being pulled in several different directions by too many people, you need to let people know that you are not going to play that game any more. A tug of war cannot take place if one person refuses to pick up that metaphorical end of the rope and pull. Think about it. Having tugs of war with important people in your life never really works, and who really needs to prove that they can come out the winner? It is an unhealthy game to get into and will always create bad feelings. So stop jumping to take responsibility every time, and see what happens.

The Guilt War

We all know this game and the terrible feelings that it evokes. Too often, people fight dirty by using guilt as a weapon. And what a fine weapon it makes. Guilt has to be one of the worst emotions to deal with. The problem with playing this game is that, not only will you feel the pain of guilt, you will also end up getting very angry and avoiding whoever is 'guilting' you. When someone makes you feel guilty, you have no status. You can't discuss matters as equals. You are the one in the wrong and you are the cause. You need to stop that game straightaway – and it begins with you making a decision. You have to take some of your power back.

Take James as an example. His mother is widowed and quite elderly. She wants him to visit every weekend. James is married with two young children and works very long hours. If he visits his mother, it takes nearly two hours to get there. He feels his mother puts a huge pressure on him, and finds it hard to juggle his responsibilities and duties. James starts to have difficulty sleeping, and decides that he can't cope any more with the guilt. He hates having to constantly refuse his mother's requests, so he decides that he will have to 'take charge' and pre-empt his mother's demands. James has come up with the idea of meeting his mother half-way every few weekends. She catches a bus and they meet for lunch or tea. He has also started breaking the routine so that his mother does not always 'expect' him to come. He phones his mother every week and, barring her being unwell or needing him, he takes more opportunities to say 'when' he is coming rather than the old way of mum saying 'I don't suppose I am going to see you this weekend – I expect you are just too busy to bother', etc. This way he has put a stop to the 'guilt war'.

An important point to remember when it comes to dealing with behaviour that affects you negatively is that often people simply don't know how to ask for what they want in a positive way. So people end up playing games (and often very negative ones rather than just being direct). So however angry you may feel, you may find it helpful to think about where they are coming from and why they do what they do.

One of the most important things to remember when it comes to your relationships is that, providing those concerned are 'adult', then they need to take their 50 per cent of responsibility in making or breaking a relationship. If you remember little else, try to hold onto that because, again, the issue of responsibility is so difficult. You cannot allow yourself to be held totally responsible for another human being – it is a dangerous position to adopt. Yes, if it is a child, or someone very mentally or physically ill, then that is a different matter, but again you would need to be careful not to remove a person's dignity by taking charge completely, or setting yourself a task and responsibility that you cannot cope with. Let's go back to your passenger list and look at your key relationships in more detail.

YOUR PARENTS

How is your current relationship with your parents? Your relationship today will be affected by the natural changes that have occurred as you have grown up and moved away from home, and also by how your parents are coping and adapting as they get older. In other words, it is a relationship that will already have had to sustain a lot of changes.

Some of you may have very elderly parents, or parents who have health problems. Do you live close to your parents or are they quite a distance away? What expectations do your parents have of you and what are you truly comfortable with? Walking around feeling that you should do more cannot be ignored. You need to ask yourself, 'why do I feel like this?', 'what do I have to do to feel differently?'.

There will also be some of you who have lost one or both of your parents. You may feel uncomfortable when you don't give yourself time to 'think' about your deceased parent, or to visit the grave or resting place. You may spend time 'talking' to them and then having periods of silence. Think about how you want to conduct your relationship. It may sound crazy, but it isn't. You can't pretend your parents didn't exist, and it will do nothing but benefit you to take the time to remember and speak to them, look at photos and videos and sometimes laugh and smile at cherished memories.

Guilt does not enhance a relationship or make it work well. Neither is it very good for your mental and physical wellbeing. So don't be lured into that trap of believing that guilt has to be a major part of your life. That will not work for you. You may not be able to make huge changes but you should not hide from attempting to do something differently. Sometimes situations seem hopeless, but rather than staying stuck in what cannot change, start to look again and see what can – it may be so minute that you hardly think it is worth doing, but do it anyway. A small change is better than no change. If you concentrate on the small changes you will often feel more able to carry them out because they are comparatively risk-free. If it does work it will give you the boost and the confidence to try and do something else. It will also give you that magical feeling that not everything is out of your control, and that really is good for the spirit.

The word 'duty' tends to crop up a lot when people talk about parents. There is nothing wrong with having a sense of duty. If you have it, it isn't going to go away, but you have to be careful what price you end up paying. If you have quite demanding parents or a lone parent, you have to decide what is realistic for you and stick to it. If you allow yourself to be either manipulated or driven by guilt you will just end up angry and resentful, feeling that you have no control over your life. In all relationships you have to consider what is OK and not OK in terms of expectations. If this is an issue that you are trying to deal with, but you just end up going back to square one, then stop now – put the book down and start to write down what you reasonably can do. That wonderful word compromise comes into our heads, and compromise is not a one-way street! (Look back at James's example.)

Things were perhaps easier in some ways when families lived very closely, often in the same town or village. When people lived like that, it was easy to maintain regular contact and share tasks like babysitting, doing Mum and Dad's garden, helping with the shopping, meeting for supper. Family life has become much more complicated because most of us do not live close enough to our parents to just 'drop in' spontaneously. Many of us will have to make a journey which may be time-consuming and tiring. If you work, your only time is at the weekends and you may feel too tired or too busy to make the trip to see your parents. Time is a very big issue for the majority of people, and therefore has a huge impact on how you deal with your own passenger list. The more you panic, feel resentful or pressurized, the less effectively you will react.

YOUR PARTNER AND FAMILY

The Pressures and Dilemmas You Face

In the second half of the 20th century, women's lives changed dramatically. They have been exposed to much choice and the expectations that result from this. How has this affected them, and how have these changes affected men, and their relationships with women? A lot of women feel very confused about what they 'should' do. Again, we want you to think about how many times you use the word 'should'. You need to be in contact with what you want and need, not living your life through shoulds. This will only lead to anger and resentment.

Some women have to work when they have children and are very troubled by this. Others choose to work, and perhaps others feel that they must work or are trapped by the financial and status rewards of their jobs. Status is a very important thing to think about. It has become more and more of an issue over the years (as we mentioned earlier) and is very much a factor in terms of how some people view themselves. When women give up work to have children, they often are faced with quite a crisis. The fact that post-natal depression is on the increase has been strongly linked to the fact that women go through such a huge change when they have a baby. There are the obvious changes of becoming a new mother, but when you team them with the fact that the new mother may have just given up work and all that it entails in terms of loss of status, identity and opportunities for social interaction, the picture becomes clearer.

Another very important issue is the impact of contraception. Years ago, women didn't have to debate about having children – it just happened! Whether or not to have children has to be one of the biggest dilemmas some women and their partners face.

It is also very important to take time to look at expectations on men. Women's lives have changed such a lot. How do men cope with this? A man brought up in a more traditional family may find dealing with the 'modern' woman quite frightening. There is also such a lack of clarity around conduct between the sexes. Many years ago it was accepted that a physical relationship would not take place in the early part of a relationship – nowadays this area is so confusing for men and women. Magazine articles have raised expectations about physical relationships when many people still find it hard to discuss difficulties or fears if they arise. A lot of women feel disillusioned that men don't treat them as if they are 'feminine', but there are so many mixed messages which probably put both sexes into a difficult and confusing place.

Finding Time for Each Other

How do you balance the time you give to your partner, children (if you have them), your work (in or out of the home) and the time you make for yourself? Time will be of particular concern to those of you who work long hours, have long journeys to work, or who are caring for children or others. How many of you arrive home in the evening feeling simply too tired to participate in family life? If your partner doesn't work, or doesn't have such a long working day, they may be feeling communicative and energetic when all you want to do is fall asleep in front of the television. What is it like if both of you commute, or if your partner stays at home looking after young children? How can you give what you don't have? How can you explain this to someone who may be feeling really ignored and unsupported because you are just too exhausted?

How can you find a suitable compromise? What is it like to come home after a long day and be criticized for not joining in family life? If you are a working parent, how much do you see your children? You probably hardly see them during the week and feel that you need some time for yourself at the weekends – but can you do that? Something needs to change but it is not that simple. As you think through these issues, please be prepared to talk about them – this will relieve your feelings of guilt and help your partner deal with their anger and resentment. Don't ignore problems. There may be no huge solution, but you can change how you feel.

For those of you who are at home with young children it may be extremely difficult to get a work-weary partner to understand how tiring your day has been and what the demands of bringing up young children are. In any relationship, it is so much better not to have competitions over who has had the worst day or who has the most demanding job. Why not simply agree to try and understand what each goes through and what it is that you need? You will experience an immediate improvement if you do.

The antidote is to talk and be prepared to listen. If the idea scares you, then try writing a letter to your partner. In it, explain how you *feel*. For example:

Dear X
I am writing to you because I am feeling very shut out and that you are constantly annoyed with me. I am not blaming you for any of this, but we are now arguing a lot and this upsets and worries me.

In the letter:

- Don't blame.
- Stick to *your* feelings.
- Offer solutions and compromises (if you can) or ask for a discussion.
- Offer to listen to them and their feelings.
- Tell them that you love them and that you want things to be different for both your sakes.

When you talk set some rules:

- No blaming.
- Say how you feel and do it in a way that the other person can comfortably hear e.g. 'I feel isolated because I know I'm at home so little' rather than 'Why can't you appreciate how hard I work? All you do is moan, moan, moan. It really annoys me.'
- Take it in turns to talk (no shouting, point-scoring, interrupting or blaming).
- Ask each other what you want. Move to a compromise, or at least be willing to do something differently.
- Don't get stuck in a rut.

Give your partner the letter and sit with them while they read it – or read it to them. Make sure you choose a suitable moment when you can have privacy and time.

YOUR CHILDREN

You will undoubtedly experience a 'tug of war' when it comes to your children. You naturally want the best for them, but your concern may come across as critical and untrusting. You may also make the mistake of assuming that you 'know and understand' your children, or believing that they will like the same things as you. To reduce the 'tug of war', start applying some of the suggestions we made about building a better relationship with your partner. Listening, showing respect and not judging will all make a positive impact.

YOUR SIBLINGS AND OTHER RELATIVES

When you look at your relationships with the rest of your family, you could be talking about quite large numbers of people. Along with your siblings and cousins, there will be their potential partners and children. The passenger list is quite likely to keep growing.

What is it you want to change about your relationships with these 'passengers'? Do you feel as the years go by that you see less and less of certain family members and that you are unhappy about that? Or do you feel that there are too many demands and pressures? Whatever you are experiencing, you need to take time to think about what it is you need and want. If it isn't happening, then do something. Also, think about the relationships from a longer-term perspective. You may be busy building a career or looking after young children, but what about later? Will you regret missed opportunities, or letting people in your wider family become strangers?

STEPCHILDREN

Many of you will have become step-parents or are in a relationship with someone who has children from a previous relationship. This is a particularly difficult area. There are support groups for families with stepchildren. People in these situations get caught up in 'shoulds', but sometimes the reality doesn't make this easy. If, for example, children are being 'difficult' it can be very hard to remain 'understanding'. You may even feel that these 'passengers' are completely unwanted but they exist and are not going to go away. In these situations it is important to be able to talk openly to someone rather than bottling it all up and exploding uncontrollably at a later date. Talking to your partner may be difficult because they will feel very torn, but do it. Do it in a way that shows you respect their feelings. It is important to be able to do a reframe. If the children are going to be in your life then viewing them as the enemy is really not going to work. Neither does that mean that you have to allow them to behave in a way that is totally unacceptable. You will have heard the word boundaries. Well, this is a good example of where they are desperately needed. You have to make allowances for very small children but there comes a time when you have to let offspring know that you expect a certain standard of behaviour and that problems need to be discussed not 'acted out'.

RELATIONSHIP EXPECTATIONS

As we said earlier in the chapter, it is very important to consider whether your 'passengers' have all read the same rule book! If we are very close to someone – married, in a stable relationship, whatever – we tend to fool ourselves over how similar we really are. Similarity is a key factor but you may be exaggerating that factor to your cost. Just because you are similar in some ways it doesn't mean you will necessarily understand each other or be able to read each other's thoughts.

Consider again your closest relationship. Have you really examined your attitudes to the roles you have in the relationship? Are you a rather traditional man (in heavy disguise) who lives with a woman who challenges you and expects the relationship to be run as a team? Or are you a guy who wants a completely equal relationship who is with a woman who expects you to be a 'hairy hunter' – the big strong man, never afraid, who will always provide, etc. What does it feel like if the combination of expectations is completely awry? Go back to your list of expectations. Be totally honest. Here are some lists supplied by several different people whom we asked at random:

Elizabeth – 35 years old

She started off by laughing and saying that she couldn't believe what she had said, and was worried about the impression she would give…

- I want my husband to provide for me so that I can stay at home with the children.
- I expect him to initiate sex, and I feel rejected and unfeminine if he doesn't.
- I expect him to be strong and competent.
- I want to be able to depend on him and respect him.
- I want him to make my life fun.

Charles – 37 years old

- I like my wife to work. She is bright and ambitious and I completely support her in pursuing her career.
- I want children with her and I understand that she will want to continue working. I can't physically make much of a contribution to the housework but I am willing to do whatever I can.
- I want us to be equals.
- I expect my wife to sometimes initiate sex.
- My wife needs to understand how important my career is and not to nag me when I am very late or have to work at weekends.

Sarah – 25 years old

- I don't want a relationship like my Mum and Dad's.
- I'd expect my partner (I don't currently have one) to listen to me and be prepared to talk things through.

- I'd want him to be able to admit that he is wrong – and I would do that too.
- I'd expect him to be completely faithful.
- I'd want him to make me feel the most important person in his life.
- I'd want him to be loving as well as physical with me.

Chris – 27 years old

- I want my partner to understand that I will share the mundane jobs around the home but I also want her to understand that I need time with my mates and don't want to be nagged when I go to the pub or to football.
- I think we should split everything 50/50 financially. I don't want children yet – in fact, I don't even know if I want them at all. So she would need to understand that.
- I don't want someone who has to analyse everything. Life is for living so I think you just need to get on with it and have a laugh.
- I'd expect my partner to be faithful and not to flirt either.

Could you imagine what would happen if Chris and Sarah got together, or indeed Elizabeth and Charles? Yet there probably are many couples whose expectations really are that glaringly different.

Whatever set of relationships you have looked into while reading this chapter, one thing is very clear. It is not always the number of passengers that are the problem – it is whether they are willing to participate in helping the driver make the journey as smooth as possible for all concerned. Think about this. There needs to be some sort of team spirit. Don't teach those around you that you will do all the work or take all the responsibility. A relationship is a two-way process. Your self-esteem will soar if you are in relationships where key people in your life value you enough to try to meet you half way sometimes. Do not be afraid to share the load – it doesn't make you weak or vulnerable, it will actually give you the time and energy to do your part really well.

Think about this in terms of your children (if you have them), or other relations. You might not be able to produce an expectation list in the same way that you would with a life partner, but it really does help to communicate with the key people in your life and talk about what is wanted and needed and whether those wants and needs can be fulfilled. Often relatives don't say 'no' to each other or explain why something isn't possible – so a war starts.

With anyone who is important in your life, it is crucial to keep the channels of communication open. If you are having a problem with your child, an elderly relative, whoever, arguing will solve nothing:

1 People don't listen when they are being shouted at or criticized.
2 You both have to talk about what it is that you want and how the other person can work towards helping you achieve that.
3 Always think about how you phrase things and work on gaining a better level of communication with the key figures in your life.

SUMMARY

- Anyone can feel that they have too many passengers. The numbers don't really matter – the feeling does.

- Feeling that there are too many pressures, too many agendas, too many people who are expressing disappointment and frustration, will grind you down. That doesn't mean that they are wrong. That is not the issue. The issue is that you will not be able to respond favourably while you feel like this. You will probably either get angry or decide to avoid the situation by shutting off, or by seeking solace in some unhelpful and damaging way.

- Remember also that where there are passengers there has to be a driver. The driver has a job to do but that does not entail doing everything for his/her passengers. There has to be co-operation, and people have to take respon-sibility for themselves as well as responding appropriately when there is genuine need.

- You need to be prepared to delegate. If there is too much to do and too little time, then something either has to 'go' or there has to be ways of sharing the load. Try to be creative with this idea rather than dismissing it by preparing a mental list of why it couldn't happen. That will just help you stay stuck and that is not why you are reading this book!

CHAPTER 5

The Corner Club

The next step is to get better acquainted with your negative thinking. This is not as ridiculous as it sounds! You need to develop a greater understanding of why you do it, as well as learning to deal with both its subtleties and full-frontal attacks. Yes, you may well know that you do think negatively, at least some of the time, but we doubt that you really appreciate the power and extent of it. You also need to realize that the first step in breaking it is facing it. In doing this you will get to understand exactly what you do. This chapter contains exercises to help you gain an even deeper understanding of your negative thinking, so that one day you can conquer it. In time you will learn to change some of those messages, deflect others and turn some into positives rather than letting them become some destructive process that simply leaves you standing on the corner watching the world go by.

This chapter is about starting to explore breaking the pattern of this behaviour, moving away from the 'corner' and concentrating on positive behaviour and the rewards of change. In order to do this you need to understand more of what you do and why you do it.

There are many people who are always waiting for the worst to happen. They seem to believe that good things don't, or won't, happen, or if they do it will not last. This negative belief system is one of the hardest to break and is a huge block to change. You can easily 'talk' yourself out of trying something, or pushing for something to happen, by saying 'it won't happen to me' or 'it won't last – good things never do'.

You may wonder why this happens. Some people will say 'Oh, I've always been this way – I was probably born like it' – well, this is not strictly true. If we were to ask you to memorize a 20-line poem, you would immediately start to protest that it would take you forever to memorize it, that you have a bad memory, etc. When it comes to things going wrong in your life, you unfortunately will have told yourself, or 'learned' exceptionally quickly, that 'these things always happen to me'. Often something only has to go wrong once or twice and you 'learn' (or you think you do) that this is what will always happen. The key to this negative behaviour is the use of 'always'. You start to 'generalize' your experiences rather than maintaining a true and realistic perspective. Or you play 'clairvoyant'. Things have gone wrong and you just 'know' in the future that they will go wrong again.

Put the book down for a second and try to trace back instances that may well have been the start of this type of process. You may be able to link experiences with 'warnings' from significant people, such as 'girls are always trouble', 'money is the root of all evil', 'don't get too big for your boots' (see also the exercise in Chapter 2 about the 'little man on your shoulder, *pages 23–4*). If you can't think of any straightaway, continue to try to remember. Your recollections could be extremely enlightening. You may also have perfectly good reasons for fearing history repeating itself – the initial experience may well have been very painful. Again, however, we must not continue to write the script that 'it' (i.e. things going wrong) has happened several times and with very important matters, and it is therefore bound to go wrong again. You may have also experienced a piece of good fortune that subsequently 'went wrong', and you tell yourself 'good things never last', or some such statement.

So how many times have you said to yourself (either out loud or internally) that 'good things never happen to me'? The next time you do it, stop. Think for a couple of minutes about whether that is really true. 'Never?' That literally means that for the whole of your life, nothing good has ever happened to you. That is almost impossible. We are not, however, disputing that you may have good reasons for feeling this way. Things may well have happened that have left this type of scar. But as we have said before, do you continue to suffer today for what happened yesterday? We hope not.

We also want you to think for a few minutes about someone you see as a successful or happy person (or both). If you were to step into that person's shoes for a moment, what thoughts do you think they would have? You may even know this person well enough to speak to them and ask them, but we bet you wouldn't hear them say things like 'good things never happen to me'. Success – professionally and personally – is as much about attitude as about skill and luck. If you believe in something strongly enough, you will help it happen. Or at worst, you will not have done something to get in the way of it happening.

So stop reading right now and just take a moment to think about one positive thing that has happened in the last seven days. Think about it long and hard. It doesn't matter if it was a small thing. Think about it, feel the feelings and tell yourself that you intend to feel this way a lot more.

Think also about whether you tend to seek the company of others who reinforce your negative thinking, or even worse, join in and amplify it.

Put the book down for a second. Think about people who are in your life and whether they are a positive or negative force. Some people may even be neutral. Are there different times in your life when you feel more drawn to some people than others? Do you, for example, have people in your life with whom you would want to discuss what you are doing at the moment? Are there people who would basically pull you back to that 'corner club' – standing on the corner watching the world go by? There may also be people who are potentially positive forces in your life and you don't know it. After all, you may need to start having different conversations with people in order to discover this. If you believe something strongly enough, you will probably generate conversations with people that simply prove what you already believe. So to get something different happening and to get people responding in a different way you need to start to talk differently.

Now we will take you step by step through your own personal process.

For the first exercise, we want you to imagine teaching someone to do exactly what you do when you think about something you want to change. So take your time and think about an example of a behaviour or situation that you would like to change. Describe it as fully as possible, as if you were explaining it to a third party. Think of the questions they would ask so that they can understand what to do to be you. This is not as crazy as it sounds as it will help you become aware of the processes, thought patterns and behaviours that you experience. If you have a trusted friend, you may even want to share this exercise.

Get your friend to ask you as many questions as necessary in order for them to be able to explain back to you exactly what you do.

You don't have to choose a scenario that is too personal, if you don't want to. Let's take Jane, for example, who works for a large software company. She has suffered from depression for a couple of years. We ask her to describe in detail what she does when she thinks about change in her life. She is quickly able to explain how she constantly feels that she wants to get away from her job. She is now quite clear that her job does not help with the depression but is also realistic that it hasn't necessarily caused it. We ask her what happens when she thinks about leaving. She is a very 'visual' person normally but explains that she sees 'nothing'. Her mental screen goes blank. (If necessary, refer back to Chapter 1 to help you with this exercise.) What happens next? 'I become anxious and tell myself that there is nothing – no future, that I am stuck.' So Jane identifies that, for her mental wellbeing, she needs to change her job, but that she cannot 'see' what it is that she can do, or what it would be like to make a change. She then becomes afraid and tells herself that she is stuck. This understandably makes her feel even more negative because the mere thought of doing something about her situation actually produces a further negative reaction. What a powerful example of how thinking about change can produce even more negative feelings.

We ask Jane to 'back up' a little bit. What information does she have that her job is affecting her health? The floodgates open. She describes how she has not enjoyed her work for years. That it gives her no satisfaction. That she dreads Sunday because it is one day closer to Monday. That she got into this line of work because she did not pursue what she originally wanted to do. On and on she goes – proving that she is totally convinced that she is unhappy at work.

But again we go back to that blank screen. This is how Jane stops herself from moving on. It puts her right back to the corner club, wishing that things could be different but not even knowing how, or where, to start. She is full of fear.

However you 'think', it is important to learn to 'see', 'hear', 'feel' and 'experience' things as clearly as possible to give you a goal to move towards. No-one can move towards a blank screen. There is nothing to motivate you. You may not be able to picture exactly what it is you want but you may see, or experience, certain fragmented ideas. Use those as building blocks. Again, people often don't move ahead because they expect to know exactly what it is that they want – well, perhaps you need to do some exploring first. You also need to appreciate that you don't necessarily have to have a total game plan.

Get yourself a piece of paper. Write down what it is you want to change. Be specific. If needs be, break it down into chunks. Don't write things like 'I want to change everything!'. That is a sure-fire way of doing nothing. Then think about what it is you want. Don't go for something that is totally impossible. Start to build a picture.

If you say 'I want to change feeling so unhappy all of the time', break this down. Focus on what is making you unhappy and on the things you can change, rather than on what cannot be changed. If, for example, you are unhappy because a loved one is terminally ill, or you have recently separated or divorced, you need to stop focusing on what can't change. That is a form of torturing yourself, and you will not move forwards if you hold on to the past or obsess about what cannot change. Ask yourself what you have stopped doing to make you feel good since all of this happened.

We spoke to someone recently who is starting to piece together what he wants. The picture is not completely clear but here are some of the things that he said. 'I have been in a very competitive field for 20 years. I was attracted by the status and the money but somewhere along the way I have changed. I realized that I am not happy – I want to work in a less competitive and ruthless job. I want to be able to use some of my skills in a different way. I really want to do something to help people. Because I am a solicitor I can perhaps change my direction but use a lot of my skills in a different way. Do something in family law, for example.'

This man has not made any decision yet but is continuing to explore. He has, however, come to a major realization. He doesn't want competition and ruthlessness any more. You too can make a start and we will show you how.

Remember that change is like a house of cards. If you change one thing it will impact on other areas of your life and other people. That is why it is so important to have a go. By doing one thing differently you can gain the strength to continue to move on and change other areas. Because of this 'house of cards' effect, it is also important that you sometimes make gradual changes so that you don't frighten yourself into a backwards turn. Here are the most important components of CHANGE:

The Five Commandments of Change

C Commitment to change
H Hard work
A Anchoring yourself – it can be easy to slide backwards
N No negatives but, yes, be realistic
G Goals
E Easy does it

Let's look now at some of the key areas in people's lives where they tend to feel the need for change, and the ways that negative thinking can block any attempt to change. So as you think about areas in your life that need to change, don't block yourself by joining that corner club. By thinking differently and being prepared to do something differently you will find that you can move on. The worst thing that can really happen is that nothing changes! You can always go back to what you have already.

MARRIAGE OR LONG-TERM RELATIONSHIP

If you feel dissatisfied in this area you may also feel completely stuck. People often don't see options other than:

1 Stay and put up with whatever the problems are.
2 Leave.

There is indeed something in between, which is basically to take action with your partner about the problems. Following this course will help you decide in which direction you ultimately need to go. There is no danger in trying. It may save the relationship or it will tell you once and for all that the relationship needs to come to an end.

First of all, whatever the problem is, ask yourself one question: is it one that you need to talk about? Don't jump in saying 'there's no point, he/she isn't going to change' etc. Answer us truthfully. Do you have anything to lose by getting honest and open and discussing it with your partner? Or to put it another way, how bad are you feeling at the moment? Can it really be made any worse by trying to do something about it? What is your fear about opening up? The only reason not to do so is if you genuinely fear violence or some such retribution. Start to confront what holds you back from doing something if you are unhappy. Don't be defeatist and say 'What's the point? It isn't going to change.'

The other thing to think about is getting some help for your relationship. There is absolutely no shame in contacting an agency like RELATE or going to see a counsellor or therapist who specializes in marital or relationship difficulties. Again, people block themselves by saying that they 'should' be able to sort problems out themselves. Why? – go on, try to answer that question – we are intrigued as to what your answer could possibly be. It doesn't make sense. If you were ill you would go to the doctor (or at least you wouldn't feel ashamed). If your relationship is 'ill' you need to go to someone who can help it.

We are sure that you have heard the rule of estate agency – location, location, location. Well, there is a golden rule to improving relationships called 'communication, communication, communication'. If you retreat from this idea, think of what will happen if you don't? Which really is worse – to say nothing and let things deteriorate further or to take a risk and do something?

Another golden rule in 'communication, communication, communication' is to learn to discuss problems without blaming, point-scoring and shaming. Think about this because it may help you have the courage to do something about your relationship. This, again, is a well-used block to change. 'How can I speak to my partner because they are going to be so hurt, or feel criticized?' Well, find a way of saying things so that you are not using criticism or blame. So just imagine for a few minutes what it would feel like to be in their shoes. You may not be able to dress things up too much but you can be respectful and try at all times to point out that your reason for saying things is because you love them and you want things to get better.

The final block to change in relationships is to trap yourself by saying 'this always happens to me. It's all my fault. All my relationships end up in disaster – I'm the one that is the problem'. What a great excuse for not discussing problems! Remember that it does take two to have a relationship. Or perhaps this is part of the problem – you don't take that into account.

If your relationship has already ended, you are bound to be experiencing some mixed emotions. If you are in a lot of emotional pain at the moment it is important not to block yourself by saying 'I'll never feel better'. Remember that you may need someone to talk to – be it a good friend or a counsellor or therapist. Most important of all, don't go condemning yourself with negative thinking. By all means take your part in the problem, but don't go taking 100 per cent.

WORK

Again, don't start by saying 'I hate my job but I can't change it because I am stuck'. You are going to have to pretend for a moment that something can be different. There is no danger in just pretending.

Answer these questions:

1. *What is happening that makes you want to change your job?*

Try and make a list of what is happening that makes you want to change your job. It may be a variety of things from boredom to ill health or anxiety. Whatever it is, write it down. Note that answering 'what' is very different from answering 'why'. We are not asking you to explain yourself or rationalize what is happening. If you go down that route, it creates another block. What you have written down becomes what you want to move away from.

The next question is:

2. *Do you have to leave your job or can something change that would make it more comfortable to stay?*
If there are possible changes, write them down, together with ideas for making them happen. Again, members of the 'corner club' tend to believe that all change has to be dramatic and huge (more wonderful blocks to change). When you attempt change on a less grand and frightening scale, your levels of motivation will rise.

If you can't identify any areas in which to make changes, then you are saying that you need to leave. Again, you need to have a strategy for finding another job. Yes, it may take time, but there is no harm in looking. What you are doing is getting in contact with choices rather than telling yourself that you are stuck. Choices will motivate you; being stuck will not. Believe us, there is no danger in exploring your options. There may be no particular job available at present but you never know when something will become available.

HEALTH

The term 'health' covers many different categories. You may simply want to get fit or you may have some medical or addiction problem that you need to resolve. On the other hand, you may have a medical condition that is serious, even terminal. If you fall into the latter category, it may be difficult for you to have any sense of motivation, but let's see what you are capable of.

If your issue is one of fitness, the first question to answer is 'what has or hasn't been happening to make me unfit?'. Take some time to answer this – you can give an off-the-cuff answer or a proper one.

What stops you exercising? What gets in your way? Why don't you take care of yourself?

As with any task, if you decide that you want to get fit then you need to break the task down into smaller tasks with shorter time limits. For example, you may set yourself the task of using an exercise bicycle for 20 minutes, three times a week. This is much better than say 60 minutes, five times a week. Don't set yourself up to fail. Also, make sure that you get some professional advice by going to a reputable gym. Lots of people miss out on maximizing their progress by not realizing that fitness and nutrition is part of a very scientific process and that small adjustments can make tangible differences.

If your concerns about your health are more serious. We want you to think about this for a few minutes. If your stock answer is 'what's the point?', try and answer that question in a very different way. Exactly, what is the point? It is a good question if you turn it around. It can apply to anyone with a serious medical condition – what is the point in looking after yourself and being as fit as you can be? In the same way, there is no age at which you should start saying things like 'it's too late' – that is just an excuse.

LEISURE AND HOBBIES

Answer these questions:

1 Do you have any hobbies?
2 When you were a child did you have hobbies?

A lot of people answer no to 1 and yes to 2.

What do you do to block yourself from having time to engage in activities that you enjoy, that help you unwind and in which you can lose yourself? We know that time can be your greatest enemy and that there are commitments that have to take a priority, but what about making a small amount of time for yourself on a regular basis? If you have a partner, you may need to discuss making it possible for both of you to have a small amount of time each to pursue a hobby.

Hobbies can be as diverse as:

Creative

- Drawing/painting
- Reading
- Sculpture
- Cookery
- Pottery
- Gardening
- Decorating

Physical

- Squash
- Tennis
- Badminton
- Football
- Cricket
- Sailing
- Walking
- Climbing
- Horse riding
- Swimming

Learning a new skill

- Language
- Writing
- Updating work skills

- Computing
- Driving
- Cooking
- Music

Spiritual/philosophical
- Yoga
- Meditation
- Collecting
- Antiques

YOUR SPIRITUAL LIFE

What do you do that really gives your life 'meaning'? What is it you do that gives you a reason to carry on and a sense of purpose? If you projected yourself to your 80th birthday party and you were telling your congregated relatives about your life, what would you want to say above anything else?

Whatever you do, don't close your mind to what gives your life meaning. It is not something wacky – it is something that strikes at the heart of why so many people are unhappy in a way that is impossible for them to comprehend. The majority of these people have no idea of what is missing. This is because they have never allowed themselves to comprehend why it is so necessary – basically, what 'it' is. We will expand further on this in Chapter 13. In the meantime, however, please give this question some thought.

SUMMARY

- You need to create a greater awareness and understanding of your 'negative voice'. By becoming more aware you can take away its power, and in time you can replace some of the negative messages with something more positive as well as realistic.

- Remember that being positive is not about being stupid or taking ridiculous risks. You need to learn not to block yourself from change by being negative. In order to build confidence in making changes you need to appreciate that you can take change stage by stage without huge risks.

- You may not be too clear about the direction in which you want to go but you are positive that you don't want to say where you are. In this case, you do need to feel your way slowly.

- As you make one small change and reap the rewards, you will naturally feel more enthusiastic and confident about having another go.

CHAPTER 6

The Posse. Who's Chasing Who?

This final chapter in your personal voyage of exploration and self-discovery addresses the need for you to learn to identify your feelings more clearly. Running away from them does not work. You can't stay permanently on the run. Even though you may tell yourself that this way works for you, you will find that you are having to pay a huge price by not listening to yourself.

Your feelings are like a barometer – perhaps not quite so scientific – but a barometer all the same. If you don't pay attention to them you are ignoring a very useful device. You can be ignoring vital warning signs as well as cutting yourself off from extremely positive feelings, if only you would allow yourself to take that risk. You may also run the risk of having to use habits or substances to enable you to continue to avoid these feelings, and this can be a price that is too high to pay. If you really want to make changes you need to be more aware of your feelings, be able to describe them more accurately and understand some of the reasons why you feel the way you do. When you do this you will be opening up a part of you that may make you feel vulnerable at the start but also very alive. Finally, it is important to remember that your thoughts drive your feelings and to realize the need to make this link. Feelings don't just arrive!

We sometimes say to clients who are always 'so busy' that it must feel like they are on the run from themselves. Running madly, afraid to stop, in case that posse of feelings should catch up with them. Some people sabotage themselves by ensuring that they always have too much to do and will never get to finish any task. This device backfires because, although you can keep yourself really busy, you also keep yourself from ever having the satisfaction of completing anything.

Let's get this into some sort of perspective. There are many people with busy lives – anyone with family responsibilities or a job will be busy. There are, however, those of you who go several stages further. You are the ones who take on so much more. You may be helping someone out with the school run (when you really don't have the time), you may have agreed to do something extra at work (that you could have actually got out of), you may be someone who refused to have help in the home or garden (even though you could find the money). You probably have lots of projects on the go and hardly any chance of completing any of them or giving them the time that you need to. As a result there may be a degree of chaos. Just think about it – you may be well organized, but if you have too many appointments on your timetable it only takes one thing to go wrong and the avalanche starts. Life in general can be like this – an avalanche just waiting to begin – and you have to work away to try and prevent it. What a state to be in. Chaos, though, is a good smoke screen. People will believe that your problem is simply that there is too much to do; they won't see what is really going on behind it.

If you can identify with this you will know that this behaviour just creates an environment of resentment and low self-esteem. How can you enjoy anything? You must feel like you are participating in some bizarre game show: constantly on the run, probably running between things that you need to do, avoiding disasters and continually clock-watching. As a result, life is a continuous uphill struggle, and that ever-present self-fulfilling prophecy that you aren't good enough because you just haven't done what you should have is chasing hard on your heels. The tragedy is that you have set yourself up to fail. If you give yourself impossible targets you will be in a perpetual state of failure. Lower your sights and you may just experience some success, which is bound to lead to a sense of motivation.

Another way of confronting this ultra-chaotic lifestyle is to ask yourself what is really going on. You are doing this for a reason. One of the most common ones is that you are literally on the run from yourself because of that posse of feelings chasing you. Not dealing with feelings is like that mountainous ironing basket, overflowing filing tray, weed-filled garden. You know they are there and you would feel better about yourself if you did something, but the task just feels too great. It's time, though, to get back in control.

Ask yourself these questions:

- How good are you at relaxing?
- Do you even know what that is any more?
- What would it be like to be with your feelings and not constantly on the run?
- When was the last time you sat still and did nothing but watch television, listen to music or talk, or shut your eyes and relax?
- Are you the sort of person who will try to do several things at once because you just can't allow yourself to have a break?

Stop for one second. Put the book down and ask yourself why don't you just stop. Put the excuses and rationalizations on one side. How afraid are you of being with yourself for any length of time? So, it's time to face these feelings and work through them, rather than run from them. This will make a huge difference to your life.

When we ask people how they are feeling, the most articulate people look at us with horror, or answer by saying 'I think'. You cannot answer the question 'how do you feel' by saying 'I think'. The problem is that the vocabulary to express feelings doesn't seem to come easily to a lot of people because most simply don't have clear and honest conversations with themselves. A lot of men, especially, have never been encouraged to talk about feelings. Think about the process of growing up. Boys are encouraged to be 'little men' and 'brave'. They are not always encouraged to talk about fear and to experience that it really is OK to talk about how they feel.

To help you develop your 'feelings vocabulary' we want you to familiarize yourself with this long list of feeling words. Please don't be insulted – we know that you know and understand these words – but we do want you to start to use them:

ABANDONED	ADVENTUROUS	AFRAID	ALONE
AMBIVALENT	ANGRY	ANXIOUS	ASHAMED
BEWILDERED	BORED	CALM	CARING
CHEATED	COLD	CONCERNED	CONFIDENT
COWARDLY	DEFEATED	DEFENSIVE	DEFICIENT
DISCOURAGED	DOWN	EAGER	ELATED
EMBARRASSED	ENERGIZED	ENVIOUS	EXCITED
FAILURE	FEARFUL	FOOLISH	FRUSTRATED
GRATEFUL	GUILTY	HAPPY	HELPLESS
HESITANT	HOPELESS	HOSTILE	HURT
INFERIOR	IRRATIONAL	ISOLATED	JEALOUS
JOYFUL	KINDLY	LONELY	LOVING
MISERABLE	NATURAL	NERVOUS	NUMB
OVERCOME	OVERJOYED	PAINED	PEACEFUL
PIOUS	PLAYFUL	PLEASED	PROUD
PROVOKED	PUT OFF	PUT OUT	REFRESHED
REJECTED	RELUCTANT	REMORSEFUL	RESENTFUL

RESPECTFUL	SECURE	SELFISH	SELF-PITYING
STUBBORN	SUCCESSFUL	SUPERIOR	SUSPICIOUS
TRANQUIL	TRAPPED	UNDERSTOOD	
UNHAPPY	UNLOVED	UNSURE	UNWANTED
UNWORTHY	USED	WARM	WEARY

The first thing to do is to start to be more aware of how you feel. When you do this, you don't have to feel that you must give an explanation. So remember that we are not asking 'why' you feel the way that you are feeling. This only leads to rationalization, which takes you away from how you feel! Also, if you constantly feel tired (in the physical sense) or listless, describe those feelings in a different way. You are simply describing your physical state, not your emotional state. Tired, for example, is a physical experience, not a 'feeling'. Keep reviewing the list and take time to consider how you are feeling. This will also help you face the things that need to change in your life. If you are not in true contact with how you feel it is extremely difficult to comprehend what things in your life need to change. In other words, you can fall into a pit of oversimplifying your problems. If, for example, you are constantly tired, there may be an obvious reason, such as your long commute every day or your broken nights with a young child, but there may also be a deeper reason.

So let's go on and look at some key feelings and get you a bit more 'feelings literate'.

ANGER

Anger can be a positive driving force or it can be turned inwards and pushed down. Remember that anger is one letter short of danger! Undealt-with anger, for example, is often a root cause of depression. If your hackles rise at this, remember that there is a world of difference between being an 'angry person' in terms of being aggressive and rude, and feeling anger. Often there is no actual display of anger because it is so heavily pushed down and controlled. Anger is also not a particularly 'pure' emotion. It is often comprised of other painful feelings, such as hurt, shame and guilt.

Women are particularly short-changed when it comes to being allowed to 'be angry'. If you think about it, little girls are socialized from a very early age that foot-stamping and other forms of anger are not very ladylike. Women therefore learn very quickly that it is not acceptable for them to show anger. Think also about the derogatory terms people have for women when they have been angry or even assertive. Rude terms such as 'bitch' and 'shrew' are often used. Aggression is seen as typically male and is therefore reasonably acceptable, providing violence is not used.

When women are angry they often cry. This leads to some very confusing feedback. How many of you identify with people commiserating with you for being upset when actually you are furious about something?

We are not suggesting that anger is something that all men are comfortable with. Many men would feel very concerned about being seen to be out of control. Others with more aggressive temperaments will be genuinely afraid of losing control and becoming violent.

Working on Your Anger

Whether you are male or female there are some very key things that you need to do with anger.

First, make a list of the things that you are currently angry about, or people whom you are angry with. Remember that there are degrees of anger, and once you have made the list you could perhaps grade it in terms of red-hot anger at one end of the scale and mild anger at the other.

When we ask you to return to this list, remember that we would expect you to start by dealing with the 'mild angers' first because this will feel safest.

Freud once likened anger to a room full of smoke. The room can hold a lot of smoke but eventually it will start to escape under the doors, through the windows, etc. This is a very good metaphor. You may have a tremendous capacity to store anger but it has to come out and will come out. That is not to say that it will burst out – it may just make you feel ill or depressed.

It is good to learn to work on angers as you identify them and experience them. This way, things don't have to get dramatic. Further on in the book we will talk more about the key of being assertive as a way of dealing with issues at the time and letting people know how you feel. One point to make at this stage is that we are not suggesting that you walk around telling people that you are angry – there are ways and means of doing it and the first point is to consider what you want to achieve by telling people how you feel. Walking up to someone and pouring out that you are feeling angry may not be conducive to a discussion which may be what you really need to have.

So go back to the list you have just written and look at a typical set of 'issues' or 'experiences' that make you angry. Often people will say 'if it's one thing that makes me really angry it's...'. Try to fill in that gap. It is useful for you to know what your sore points are.

Anger Sometimes Masks Hurt

You also need to be aware of what may be hurting you. People so often express anger as the predominant emotion because they would become too vulnerable if they admitted that they were hurt. We do not want to admit to ourselves that people can have that power over us. To be 'hurt' by someone emotionally is an awful feeling and, yes, a natural reaction is to be angry with the person who has hurt us. Again, a key point is to learn to check out with people (if it is safe for you to do so) what their intention was. Say, for example, you felt that someone seemed abrupt with you and that their reaction was unnecessary and hurtful, you should go and 'check it out' with them. You don't have to march up to them and say 'I thought you were abrupt two minutes ago and I'm angry with you', but you can say 'when we spoke two minutes ago I felt that you didn't want to talk and I am concerned as to why that is'. This gives the person the opportunity (without attacking them) to answer and perhaps explain. So often people seem to be negative towards us when it may be that they have a problem or are distracted by something which has nothing to do with us. We may just happen to get on the receiving end of their feeling.

SHAME AND GUILT

We have already talked a lot about guilt. To explain the difference between guilt and shame let's put it simply. Guilt means that 'I have done something wrong', and shame means that 'there is something wrong with me'. Both feelings are probably the most uncomfortable and awful feelings that you can have, and will certainly make a very powerful posse. In an attempt to escape these feelings it is quite common for people to drive themselves hard in order to prove themselves or to redress some real or imaginary balance. Let's now look at these two emotions separately.

Guilt

If you are feeling guilty it can be as a result of many different things. You may have deliberately done something 'wrong'; you may have purposely hurt or wronged someone; you may have wronged or hurt someone unintentionally; or it may be more subtle and perverse – that something good has happened in your life and you feel that you don't deserve it (this is more of a self-esteem issue but the tangible feeling will be one of guilt). It may go even deeper. You may always feel guilty and cannot remember a time when you didn't. It may even be that 'guilt' is part of your family culture.

The first of these guilty feelings may be difficult to resolve. You may need to try to understand why you took the course of action that you did. Our job is not to give you excuses. It feels better to be prepared to take responsibility, and when you do this you can then decide if you want to move on. This brings us on to the question of whether you should make amends for a 'wrong doing'. There are some key points:

- Would there be repercussions on you that would make such a step a negative one?
- Would you hurt the 'wronged' person further if you tried to make amends?

Think about these things. Sometimes people want to rush in to make amends when it is not the best course of action. Sometimes it can be a selfish act – you want to get something off your chest and you are not considering how the other party will feel.

Shame

Shame, as we said earlier, is about saying to yourself 'there is something wrong with me'. This can happen for all sorts of different reasons.

Something may have happened to you, some sort of abuse, for example. When bad things happen to you or around you it is natural, unfortunately, to blame yourself in some way; to ask yourself 'what did I do?', 'why did this happen to me?'. Abuse can be physical, psychological, sexual or verbal, or a combination of these. Remember that you do not have to compare yourself to others. If you have been shamed in some way then do not try to whitewash it or negate your feelings. This is a very powerful feeling and a very destructive one.

Anxiety

This emotion can run from being a mild irritant to a totally disabling condition. We don't have to describe the feelings of anxiety; you know them and you know what it feels like psychologically and physically. You need to realize, though, that you don't have to let anxiety rule your life. Later on in the book we will talk more about learning to face your fears gradually, and thus begin to conquer your anxiety.

It is important to be aware that anxiety has a flip-side to it. It is about really wanting something. Think about being anxious about exams. You are anxious because you really want to pass. Similarly, being anxious about a job interview happens because you want the job. Don't confuse anxiety with excitement. That might sound really crazy, but the sensations are very similar, and if you do suffer from anxiety then you can end up labelling everything as anxiety. So the next time you feel 'anxious', stop and check out with yourself what is really happening – what it is you are really feeling.

You also need to be wary of the complex layers of feelings that can cause self-destructive behaviour patterns. As we said earlier, anger can be a positive driving force or totally destructive. The choice is yours. Again, you may feel 'angry' at this statement – stop, think, be prepared to listen. You do have some choice in how you feel. In fact, you have more choice than you realize. If a major tragedy has occurred in your life, we are not about to tell you that you can choose to feel happy while you are in the midst of terrible pain. That would be ridiculous. But under less painful and tragic circumstances you do need to start to believe that you have a choice.

We are speaking more about day-to-day life and the choices that you have available to you. If all you do is run from your feelings you will never begin to experience what you can do to make a positive contribution to how you feel. Remember that your thoughts drive your feelings. If you walk around feeding yourself with negative messages, then guess what? You are going to feel bad. If you go one step further and get as out of contact with how you feel as possible, then you often can't even explain to yourself 'what is the matter?'. You actually don't know because you are on the run and trying not to think about what is really going on within you.

You need to face yourself with the belief that there is a healthier and more positive way out. We are not talking miracles but about doing something that can make a huge difference to your life. Before you go on to the next chapter, we want you to reread these last few paragraphs. We want you to really think about what they are saying and how you can start to apply it to yourself.

SUMMARY

- Remember that you need to stop being on the run from your feelings. If that posse is chasing you, then you need to stop and face whatever it is.

- By doing this you will create a sense of control in your life rather than living with the chaos that running always brings. You will also find that the chaos will attack every positive fibre in your life because nothing will ever really go well, or go well for long.

- Facing yourself will help you make changes because you will truly be in contact with how you feel and what needs to change.

- You also need to get things in perspective. Don't run your life fearing that you have too much going on so if one thing goes wrong it will spell disaster.

- You need to consider taking time for yourself – stop making excuses.

- Stop being afraid of your feelings – let them work for you.

How to Make Changes

CHAPTER 7

The Simple Fact of Truth

You have already done a lot of work in gaining a greater understanding and awareness, and this next stage will consolidate what you have done so far. This chapter is the first in Part II of the book, which shows you how to start making changes. This chapter will focus you particularly on making an inventory – including both positives and negatives – which makes the platform from which changes can begin.

It is easy to be self-critical, or focus on what isn't happening or going right. This process can become yet another powerful block to change. The inventory will force you to confront changes that you know perfectly well need to happen but keep getting put on the back-burner. Some of these are bound to fall into the health category. Remember it is extremely difficult to find the resources to make changes if you have health problems, be they physical or mental, or if you are struggling with an addiction. It is ridiculous for you to consider changes in all other areas in your life when there is a glaring problem that will always dominate. This inventory will also, therefore, help you see where your priorities lie in making changes, as well as whether your plan involves challenges that need to be dealt with in any particular sequence. Finally, you may be helped by grading your challenges in terms of difficulty and risk, so that you can be sure to start off by practising on those that rank quite low.

We hope that you have spent a good amount of time on the last chapter – giving yourself enough time to get really acquainted with the 'feeling' words and starting to apply them. As you do this, begin to notice what happens. Doesn't it feel a bit different, for example, to stop saying things like 'I'm tired' and actually bothering to go that bit further and ask yourself what is really happening, that is, how you are feeling? So, as you continue to understand more about how you are feeling, you can actually start to do something about the negatives, as well as learning to utilize the positives. Also, how can you know where to begin changing if you don't even know what is really going on, and how can you maintain change if you are not aware of potential difficulties and give them some consideration at the outset?

Before you go any further with the idea of making changes, we must point out that we don't want you to fall into the trap of wanting or feeling that you have to change everything. No-one needs to change 100 per cent, and if you begin with that attitude, you will quickly experience that familiar lethargy and give up. And why wouldn't you? Don't build a mountain for yourself and expect to feel excited about climbing it! Break whatever changes you are thinking about making into smaller components and tackle each bit one at a time.

Let's give you Mike as an example. He hates his current job but has good job security which he doesn't want to relinquish. He also really likes the team that he works with and would feel disloyal to them if he left. He wants to move to the country and commute to work but he thinks his bosses will object because they like him to be 'on call' at all times. He really is unhappy with where he lives and feels that, if this could change, he would cope better with work.

Mike wants to charge in to work and lay his cards on the table. He forecasts that his idea will be vetoed, that there will be a confrontation and he will be asked to leave. We suggested to him that he stop being a 'bull in a china shop' and think about approaching the problem in a slightly different way. We suggested, for example, that he start house-hunting, put his home up for sale, and then take things stage by stage. It may be quite a few months before he even finds a property, and then several more before he would move. This way he is buying time, and he is also starting to set his plan in motion. This will also give him time to consider if there are any further options or anything that he would want to change in his original plan. Most important of all, he is doing something that will alleviate a lot of his anger and resentment and will prevent him from doing something too drastic. This way he really has nothing to lose. At this stage there is no point in telling his bosses anything because nothing is concrete yet.

DOING AN INVENTORY

We now want you to take a good look at yourself. You need to explore and examine all aspects from the physical through to the emotional, mental and psychological. Don't forget that the inventory needs to include your good points, and the not-so-good. So write down the pluses and minuses. Don't delude yourself, but don't beat yourself up either.

So let's begin the thorough inventory. As you work on this, you will need to consider the things about yourself that you might want to change. Yes, it's okay to want to make physical and health changes, but also think about you – the inner you. You may, for example, want to work on changing your assertiveness, or the way you deal with anger, or you may want to learn some new skills to enhance either work or your personal life. You may want to concentrate on your spiritual life. Be really confrontational with yourself. If that list gets halted by a loud voice that says 'what's the point?', then quickly ask yourself whether you want to continue to listen to voices that hold you back, or are you going to give yourself permission to forge ahead? Start by being in charge of your life. We want you to be realistic with the changes you want to make, but we don't want you to underachieve either. Give yourself permission this minute to go in search of your true potential. You also need to feel in control and on top of things, and you don't have to be a control freak to achieve this! Start to get excited about your unused talents. Finding them could bring you more than you could ever imagine.

Get yourself a blank sheet of paper. Jot the following headings down:

- Physical health
  - Addictions
  - Food and weight issues
- Mental health
  - Mood
  - Worries and personal difficulties
- Your spiritual life
- Skills

Read through the following section, which contains questions and pointers to help you to formulate your inventory. Then start to fill in your observations, thoughts and goals.

Physical Health

When was the last time you had a check-up? When was the last time you went to the dentist? If you have any on-going medical problems, are you up-to-date with the care that has been prescribed? If you are overweight, drinking too much, working too hard, have any nagging health concerns, then you need to get really honest with yourself and do something. If you block yourself by saying 'it's too late to sort my health out' or conjure up the worst possible diagnosis, this needs to be confronted. If you think the worst, then you have nothing to lose by finding out for real! If you think you can't improve your physical or mental condition then, again, you have nothing to lose. We appreciate that some of you reading this may well have serious health problems, even terminal illnesses. We hope that you will resolve to maintain your health and wellbeing to its greatest capacity for as long as you can.

The next step is to take your goal one stage at a time. You can only feel better about yourself if you take action. Thinking about things will get you nowhere. If, for example, you are overweight, then what are you prepared to do about it? There is no point in doing something because someone else tells you to do it. This will just breed resentment and you won't continue. Stop. Put the book down and get really honest with whatever the problem is. Write it down and think about the consequences – those that you are experiencing right now, and those that you think may come later. If you are, for example, two stone overweight but just aren't prepared to face dieting for the next two to three months, then ask yourself what you are prepared to do? Make a start somewhere. For example:

- If you can walk to work, or at least part of the way, then do it.
- Cut out snacks.
- Cut out a few high-calorie foods, such as chips and chocolate.

Whatever you decide, be specific – you must have a plan. For instance, 'I will walk to work three times a week for a month.' If the weight starts to come off, you may then find the motivation to move up a gear. This is the same with many problems. So don't go for the mountain. Go for breaking the challenge down. What is better – that you stay the same weight or lose two pounds over time?

A lot of people take their health for granted and can often ignore warning signs. The benefits of being 'fit' are remarkable and far-reaching. We are not talking about having a 'washboard' stomach or bulging biceps. Just being 'fit'. One benefit of getting fit is that your ability to cope with stress is immediately improved. Exercising also helps your concentration. You don't have to 'pump iron' – you could just take the dog for a brisk walk on a regular basis. Again, don't block yourself by deliberately setting the goal too high. Do what you can – little is better than nothing. This does not mean, by the way, that you can't continue to increase your expectations, just aim to achieve one goal, and maintain it for a while before setting a more challenging one. Most important of all, create an attractive 'picture' or dialogue, or feeling, so that you can feel enticed and excited, or at least reasonably positive!

Addictions

Your inventory may include looking at your use of alcohol and drugs. People often ask us what constitutes a drink or drug problem. The answer is simple. Be really honest with yourself – if your drinking or drug-taking is causing you, or those around you, 'problems' then you are in trouble with it. If you are also experiencing any type of withdrawal symptom, such as shaking and sweating, or feelings of panic the morning after 'using', then you are in even greater trouble. You probably have a physical addiction. This means that you may end up having to 'use' in order to counteract the withdrawal symptoms. This becomes a very dangerous cycle.

People with drink or drug problems are quite rightly told either to cut right down or to stop completely, depending on whether they are 'addicted' or not. Those who are told to stop completely hardly ever do that straightaway. Why? Because adults need to feel that they can make up their own minds about things; if not, the first reaction is often to rebel. But who are you rebelling against, and who are you actually going to hurt? If you are worried about your use of alcohol or drugs, you need to get expert help. The first thing to do is be really honest with yourself and decide what steps you are willing to take. Don't hear this as some escape clause. It isn't. What we are saying is that you must do the footwork and then get help. If you insist on doing it on your own then you need to be honest about the goals that you set yourself. If you say 'I am going to cut my drinking down', then be specific. If you don't achieve this and maintain it, then you need help. Also, you need to be careful about stopping any drug (including alcohol) abruptly. To do this you need to consult your general practitioner and be honest with your doctor about what you are using.

Food and Weight Issues

We have already mentioned weight as a health issue. It is also important to mention it as part of an eating disorder. (The two are very different and people with eating disorders should not see a 'diet' as a solution – if anything, it can just become part of the problem.) If you regularly do any of the following, then you need help: binge, starve, vomit, abuse laxatives, eat all day, obsess about your weight, use exercise in an obsessive way. Do not accept the unacceptable. Do not believe that you are stuck like this. You can make changes – thousands of people do so every year. Eating disorders are serious and you know in your heart when you are in trouble, even if you are not admitting it to anyone else. Admitting that you have a problem and being willing to do something about it is the first step in dealing with it.

Before you go any further, we want you to take stock of how much your 'use' of drugs, alcohol, food – either one of them or a combination – is getting in the way of you leading a happier and healthier life. These questions will help you think quite specifically:

1 How often do you feel very unwell after an alcohol or drugs binge? OK, some people can go overboard just once in a while, but beware. Do you feel shaky, sweaty, too ill to go to work or too ill to work effectively? This is more than just a bad hangover. If you abuse food, how do you feel the next day – are you drained and exhausted and have to make excuses to get out of going to work?
2 Do you spend a lot of time thinking about drugs, alcohol or food, and perhaps sneaking around in order to use, drink or eat in secret?
3 If you try 'white knuckling' and don't use for a while, how do you feel? Do you feel distracted and desperate?
4 Is your 'use' of alcohol, drugs or food affecting your relationships to the point that your behaviour is causing concern to those closest to you?

If you are concerned about these issues, please consult the Resources section at the back of the book for a list of suggested reading and some telephone numbers of organizations that can help you.

Mental Health

The words 'mental health' usually make people feel very uncomfortable, but your mental health is as important as your physical health. If there is something getting in the way of this, then you must take action. Stop for a moment and ask yourself whether you have any concerns. You can grade your concerns from slightly concerned to very concerned. Mark these on a scale of 1–10, with 1 being the lowest. Issues to consider are as follows.

Moods

We are not asking you to self-diagnose but you do need to ask yourself: 'How debilitating are my moods?'. Everyone experiences low moods and anxiety at stages in their lives, but if you literally can't get out of bed, if you dread the future, feel absolutely sick with fear and possibly have panic attacks, get straight to your doctor. Do not live with the unacceptable. Your doctor can assess your condition and decide whether or not you need medication. But also ask about the availability of counselling or therapy. If your moods are not quite so severe, and you know what is contributing to them, then you need to make a list – if you don't, you are in a no-win situation. Don't ignore matters that are affecting you badly, even if you are unsure as to how you could resolve them. People have often come to speak to us about matters like relationship problems, bereavement, coping with addicted partners, work issues – the list is quite endless.

Whatever the problem is, ignoring it or being angry about it will not do any good. You will also benefit by doing something – a point to which we keep coming back.

Worries and Personal Difficulties

The range of things that you can worry about is enormous. If you are genuinely worried about something, ask yourself 'what can I do?'. If you can do something, then you need to prepare an action strategy. If you have worries that need an input from a professional, such as debt, then make an appointment and do it now! You would be surprised how many people tell themselves that they should be able to resolve their problems when they simply don't have the skill or expert knowledge.

There are also worries that are never going to be resolved. You may be in a situation where there is really nothing that you can do. We don't need to tell you how horrible that feels – you are living it. To save your sanity and mental wellbeing, you need to start to focus on other things, particularly things that you can change. It does not matter how small they are – you need a sense that there is something in your life that you can control. We are not suggesting that you stop seeking solutions to big problems but there is no point in just dwelling on them. That becomes almost like a form of torture.

One of the major sources of worry has to be around relationships. We have already talked a lot about relationships but now it is time to take stock in a slightly different way. If there are problems, it is now time for you to commit to doing something, unless of course you are willing to continue living with the problem. The problem may be affecting you too much, in which case you cannot continue with whatever it is. To help you commit and feel more comfortable, ensure that you are not thinking in black-and-white terms. When relationships go wrong (for whatever reason) there are more than two solutions – stay or leave. Leaving is not really a solution – it is a statement that nothing can be done. For more on this, look back to Chapter 4.

Your Spiritual Life

We find that a lot of people confuse spirituality with religion. Spirituality and religion are worlds apart. Spirituality is a feeling; it's a sense of goodness and wellbeing that we all have inside of us but, sadly, we are often not in contact with it. It can come from all sorts of different sources. You can be moved by the beauty of nature, a piece of music, a loved one, but the feeling is unmistakable and creates a sense of 'that's what my life is really about', 'this is why I am here and I can enjoy my life'.

Start to think about your spiritual life. We will come back to this issue later on in the book.

Skills

You may want to think about your skills in your inventory. If so, you will need to break them down into different categories. You may be thinking about work skills, personal skills, skills related to a pastime or hobby. Think really hard about the pluses and minuses, and what it is you want to change.

Don't fall into the trap of thinking that you 'should' know something or have a certain skill. One of the most important things at this stage is to be able to say to yourself 'I don't know', or 'I can't do it by myself'. Give yourself both the permission to learn and the permission to seek professional help and advice.

Other Matters

On a basic level, you also need to think about that familiar list of things that you would do if only you had the time. It could be going to the dentist. It may be home filing. It may be ringing people. Take the plunge and write down all the things that you know need doing and start working on them now. Some things on the list may only take a matter of minutes. If you whittle this list down you will feel more able to move on. It doesn't matter how long the list is – psychologically you will feel better if you are simply making a start. Start right now.

Also, don't discount pluses because you feel they have brought you nothing positive. We very sadly recall a former colleague who once said 'I see no point in being nice. It doesn't do me any good'. By using this book effectively you should find that doing a few things differently will actually bring great changes – you may only have to invest a little to reap a substantial reward.

This chapter has been about the need for you to not only be aware of, but also to commit to, what needs to change. You have to get to the action stage even if you are unsure exactly where it will lead you. Seeking advice, for example, carries no risks other than a reality check and you have to allow yourself to obtain information that may well begin to generate the extra motivation you need. Once you have begun to face the things that you want to change you need to start to demonstrate this in your behaviour and attitude. No matter how false it may seem, you need to act 'as if' it really is going to work this time. Finally, another key factor is that the formula to success may have some concrete pointers but it is also up to you to create your own individual and personalized formula. This ensures a greater likelihood of success. You also need to prioritize.

SUMMARY

- Don't go for mountains. Go for breaking the challenge down into smaller components. If you are setting an initial time-frame, then commit to a small amount of time; when you have achieved it, simply re-commit.

- Don't block yourself with hunting for the 'perfect solution'. You haven't found it so far so learn to find your own way and do it stage by stage.

- You have a right to change. Get angry about what you are denying yourself.

- Don't call problems 'problems'; call them challenges.

- Don't look at solutions and try and make them fit you. Allow yourself your individuality. You will feel more committed if you are comfortable and believe in the solution.

CHAPTER 8

Spot Your Driver

Who really is in charge? If you don't feel that you are then it is time to take charge and do some things differently. One powerful way of achieving this is to identify what drives you and get really honest with yourself. Your drivers are powerful forces that need to be understood and harnessed to make them work effectively and productively. If not, they can hinder you or propel you backwards. So you need to take charge of them. But don't get into that driving seat without knowing the destination and route that you need to take. Be clear, specific and don't be thrown off-course by low self-esteem, doubt or negativity. Who says you can't succeed? What proof do you have? What's wrong with having to learn to do something differently? Get in control. You are ultimately the one who steers the course. It's too precious to give it second best. It's too important not to give it your time and energy.

The key theme of this book is identifying your 'drivers'. Drivers can motivate you or de-rail you as they are powerful internal forces that need to be understood and harnessed in order to drive you forwards, avoiding the ones that can drive you back to square one. There are many types of drivers; you will find that you need to separate out the positive from the negative. We will not be able to list them all, but we will take you through some of them.

We liked the concept of 'drivers' because of Beechy's own battle with addiction, which thankfully ended 17 years ago. We were thinking about the times when he was so self-destructive. It became really clear that he was 'driven' in one direction only and that was destruction and negativity. He would sabotage every good thing that anybody was trying to do for him. He would turn everything around to the negative. Consequently, all he ever got was negativity. Now, you could say that the reason he behaved like that was because of the alcohol and drugs he was taking at the time. But the reality was that the behaviour was more about him than the substances he was using. With or without the substances, this tendency or 'driver' existed. So today, he still has to be very careful. Just because he is not using alcohol or taking drugs doesn't mean to say that he won't behave in a negative or destructive pattern. At all times, he has to take responsibility for the way he behaves and for the way he drives himself.

Taking responsibility is something that you are going to have to learn to do if you want to improve the quality of your life. If you are having problems, if you continually 'drive' yourself in a negative or destructive way, then you have to do something about it and you have to do something about it today. No matter what has happened in the past, the only person who can make or break today is you. So don't keep having to pay for others' bad behaviour or mistakes. Don't be driven negatively by your past. Turn it around and let it propel you forwards, and in time it will set you free. Think about it: if you fill today with all sorts of positives – from people in your life to experiences you may have – you decrease the amount of room you have to hold onto the past. If you are 'busy' with today and have to give it a lot of thought, then your mind can't keep wandering back, unless you want it to.

We want you now to take responsibility and have a good, honest look at what is driving you. We don't mean a half-hearted look at this. You need to be vigorously honest. If you are not going to do this, you will not be able to effect any changes or get any long-lasting happiness and change in your life because certain drivers will simply push you back to where you started. These will include drivers that don't allow you to take risks, and basically keep you sticking with the familiar. They may, therefore, be disguised as 'safety' drivers, or damage-limitation drivers. Try and remember this saying: 'keep doing what you are doing and you are going to keep getting what you have already got'. If what you have is okay, then put this book down and give it to someone who needs it more than you! If what you are getting at the moment is not good enough for you, then let's get serious.

Do not avoid drivers because you don't like to admit what motivates you. If your driver is 'financial', then be honest. If you find that your driver is more about human needs, again be honest, even if it makes you look at the appropriateness of what you do. This book is all about taking up that challenge rather than running from it. So don't hang on to something at all costs. Your happiness and mental and spiritual wellbeing are worth more than that.

Can you spot any of your drivers among these?

- Positive driver
- Negative driver
- Fearful driver
- Angry driver
- Lonely driver
- Loving driver
- Trusting driver
- Exciting driver
- Spiritual driver
- Status driver
- Self-esteem driver
- Financial driver

- Power driver
- Authoritative driver
- Competitive driver
- Defensive driver
- Relationship driver
- Sex driver

Perhaps work is one of your biggest drivers? People derive so much status and self-esteem from their work and it becomes a trap. They need work to feel good about themselves and therefore miss out on achieving this from other sources. In other words, you can stop investing healthily in other areas of your life because of the power of one driver, and what happens if a problem occurs in that area?

DRIVERS IN DISGUISE

You also need to watch out for drivers that are disguised! These can endanger your progress by pushing you in totally the wrong direction. You may not think about resisting because drivers are so powerful.

Take anxiety for example. As we mentioned in the Introduction, anxiety is not what it appears. Say, for example, that you are anxious about a project at work. The anxiety lies in the fact that you want the project to be successful. You want it to go well. You are therefore anxious about something not turning out positively. Anxiety, however, tends to hook you into the awful feeling that it evokes. You know, the stomach churning, sweating palms, and the negative messages that accompany it. For example, 'I know this isn't going well', 'I am sure there must have been something else I could have done', 'I just don't think I have done my best and it is going to be found out'. If anxiety is really recognized for what it is, it is possible to turn it around so that it drives you forwards. You know there is a world of difference between playing those familiar anxiety tapes in your head and saying to yourself that 'I really want this to go well'. Say that a few times to yourself and see how it feels. Yes, it feels quite different from when you are being driven by the negatives.

One further point is that anxiety-prone people also tend to label all sorts of different experiences as anxiety. It becomes an umbrella term. Think about excitement for example. Excitement actually feels very similar to anxiety. Yes, your stomach churns, the heart beats faster, you may sweat a little. So don't confuse anxiety with excitement. What a huge mistake that would be. Excitement is a very positive driver. Anxiety in its raw form is not. Please stay aware of this.

USING YOUR DRIVERS

Once you start training your mind to spot the driver you are experiencing, it will become very easy for you to get in contact with your feelings and to know whether you are behaving in a positive or negative way. Identifying your drivers therefore alerts you to think about what is currently motivating you, and can therefore act as a gauge to measure the appropriateness of your behaviour. Once you are able to do that, you will start to behave very differently. Think about an angry confrontation with someone. Stop for one second before you react and consider why it is necessary to be driven to try and prove a point when the other person is not going to listen anyway. Have you ever noticed what happens when people argue? Everybody talks at once and no-one listens. That can only lead to a totally redundant behaviour that ends up with two people yelling and screaming at each other and no-one getting anywhere. And remember, when you get angry, it takes quite a lot of energy. So why not put that energy into a behaviour that is going to be worthwhile for you rather than wasting it on negative behaviours? Don't be 'driven' to win when there is nothing for you to gain! It will simply end up being a Pyrrhic victory.

Spotting your driver is partly an intuitive thing. It can help if you picture what you are thinking. So let's take the scenario of having a task to do. It could be at work or at home. How many times do you get into the frame of mind that you can't or won't do it? You may even start making up excuses as to why you can't do it. The chances are that you can because either you wouldn't have been asked to do the task or would not have thought of tackling it in the first place. How many times do you go to start something and then talk yourself out of it? If you manage to convince yourself that you can't do it, you will be left feeling inadequate. Not only that, you will also be very angry because you know deep down that you can do it. Most times, tasks aren't completed because of a fear that seizes you and tells you that you can't do it, or that it won't be very good, or you will fail. Remember, though, that good feelings come from the completion of a task. So again, if you break the task down into stages, you will have opportunities along the way to affirm yourself and say 'yes, I've completed stage one' or whatever. If you buy into that fear, it will start to control you – it can become a very negative driver. Fear can also be a device used by some people to propel them into action at the last minute. If you feel that you have to do something, you are very likely to see that it happens. Also, think about how easy it is not to do something if you don't make a tangible commitment. If you do this, than you will allow some powerful drivers to kick in, such as 'obligation' and 'duty'.

Let's just recap on the process of using your drivers effectively:

1 Confront the task.
2 If you think about what could go wrong – ask yourself what negative drivers are in play?

3 Challenge the negative thinking and get in contact with your positive drivers, such as 'excitement', 'work', 'challenge', 'achievement'...
4 Make a commitment – this will wake up several potential drivers such as 'obligation', 'duty', 'competition', 'fear of failure' (a driver that clearly can be used positively).
5 Break the task down into stages so that you can drive yourself on each time you have completed another portion. This will help you access your 'confidence', 'self-esteem' and 'satisfaction' drivers.

CONFRONTING NEGATIVE DRIVERS

You need to decide right now to stop being driven by negatives. Put the book down and think of all of the times you have talked yourself out of doing something. Remember that there really is no-one else doing it. Sadly, it will have been you stopping yourself from doing something that deep down you really know you can do. So, write a list of those situations that have happened recently and, if possible, go back as far as you can remember. In this way you can look at the history of your negative self-talk. Why not start to get annoyed about this thief – this spectre that steals opportunities from you?

Doing this should help you to quickly build a picture of what has been happening. By recognizing the negative effect this has had, and by confronting these drivers, you will be getting out of the way of yourself. Also, don't be seduced by thinking that it is okay to have some sort of 'protective' driver – caution is fine but it should not get in the way of you living. If you keep doing this you are being your own worst enemy. You are the one who stops you doing the things that you want to do – and why shouldn't you do them? Take a risk. In fact, start taking some big risks. Put all of this fear into perspective. Fear is just 'false evidence appearing real' – **F E A R**.

We talked in the Introduction about this false evidence and we now want you to think a bit more about it. So think of a scenario when you have had to do something that you were afraid of, but you did it and did it well. No doubt you will have felt fearful and anxious (in the negative way!). You will have started to 'picture' the worst that could happen – 'supposing this goes wrong…'. As you continued to build the pictures you would have been filling yourself with 'false evidence'. It was false evidence because it hadn't happened. You were projecting. Yes, you may reflect on past experiences that have gone wrong but there is nothing to suggest that history has to repeat itself. You can decide to picture something positive – that would be as 'real' as picturing something negative. You are not a clairvoyant so you cannot predict, but you can choose to fill yourself with some positives. You won't have anything to lose. As we've said before, we are not asking you to become reckless, we are just suggesting that you do some things differently and see how you feel about the outcome. If you don't like what happens you can always go back to your old ways!

Remember, also, that we are not saying that anxiety, or you being nervous, is totally negative. There is a saying that 'if you are not nervous it's not working'. You don't have to be too comfortable. Always have a little bit of nervousness – it will keep you right on the edge and alert. It will help you. Fear is a very different thing, and filling yourself with it will cause all sorts of complications. So let's go back to that scenario and move you to the end when the task is completed successfully. Didn't you think afterwards 'what on earth was I worrying about?', 'what was all that fear about?', 'what was all that anxiety about?'. You know that you can fill yourself with 'false evidence' and it just gets in the way. It's such a negative driver. We really want you to be aware of this one because it is all important. What you have been doing is 'projecting' negativity, which is another strong driver that gets totally in the way of making progress and depletes your motivational resources.

LIVE FOR THE MOMENT

One of the greatest difficulties human beings have is staying and living in the moment. Living within the day. We so often tell people we work with that they need to just concentrate on the next 24 hours. Just keep things right in the moment. Don't obsess about tomorrow. (Okay, we know that there are practical plans that may have to be made, and it is good to have goals and dreams, but other than those try focusing on the here and now – not looking back and not looking forward, unless it is to think about something really pleasant.) The only reference that you really have is yesterday. You don't know at all what is going to happen tomorrow. But once you fall into projecting negatively, everything in the future can look glum. Just think about that for a moment. Think about what you are doing. You are saying to yourself 'this, this and this' is going to be awful when you don't even know what is going to happen. It sounds really silly, doesn't it? In fact, it sounds grandiose to believe that you do know when actually you don't. It is a redundant behaviour that will bring you nothing but more negativity.

FIGHTING LOW SELF-WORTH

Please don't get the impression that we think you are doing anything wrong. There is no right or wrong way. You can, unfortunately, blame yourself when it isn't your fault – you may not be aware of what you are doing, or you don't believe in yourself. Let yourself off the hook for a moment. This chapter is about you making some big changes in your life. So don't start projecting negativity – that you can't, or that you are not worth it, or that you don't have the intelligence. In other words, watch out for that low self-worth driver. 'I am not worth doing this for', 'I'll never be asked because I'm not worth it'. Well, you are worth it. There is no-one that isn't worth it. Someone said to us recently 'God doesn't make nobodies, everyone is somebody'. Everybody has got an identity. Everybody has a personality. Everybody has skills and talents. The problem is that a lot of people don't recognize them and use them. A lot of people don't look for the good things and qualities that they have. The main reason for that is because they get caught up in low-self worth. Also, many people are brought up 'not to show off', and this often has a bad effect and creates a very negative driver – there is a difference between humility and feeling unworthy.

Unworthiness is a really negative and destructive driver. It causes all sorts of problems. It can cause people to believe that change for them is simply not possible and, what's more, is undeserved because they feel so bad about themselves. They feel isolated and alienated, and it gets so dark and lonely that they can't talk to anybody and tell them how they are feeling. They become depressed and simply can't see any way out.

Sue, a 30-year-old advertising executive, talks about her frightening symptoms:

The symptoms of my depression once I reached my 'full stop' last September were an inexhaustible desire to sleep (in the hope that it may all be better tomorrow), crying, a racing brain, sickness, loss of appetite and, biggest and most gruesome of all, FEAR. Fear of being attacked in the street, fear of nasty or hurtful things being said, fear of eating too much, fear of the phone, fear of working, fear of other people's opinions, fear of losing my job and, more predominantly, fear of myself.

There are countless thousands of people who are feeling like that and they don't know why. You may be among them. Can you identify with it? Can you feel the need to change it? To escape feelings like this you need to be able to turn things around and change the drivers. Don't let those 'people' in your 'car' any more. In other words, don't let those negative thoughts get a hold of you.

Sue continues about her low self-worth driver and her subsequent plunge into depression:

On the work front my boss made me feel that my best was never good enough. I would work long and arduous hours, and endless time was spent theorizing on how I could improve myself. When I needed my boss's support he chose to ignore my loyalty and hard work. Although feeling terribly let down and embarrassed by what had happened, I had to rethink my position. I needed to realize that my hard work hadn't achieved much other than to increase the company's success and my exhaustive state.

Sue left her job, and after several months of being too ill with depression to work, she resumed her career, but has reassessed her attitude to work:

I needed to create a balance between work and me. Work, when all is said and done, is the means to a life, but is not a life.

In other words, Sue is not looking to get all her self-worth from work and she is wary of her 'work' and 'self-esteem' drivers. She has come to realize that she must find a balance. If she doesn't achieve that, the price is going to be too great.

John is a 35-year-old teacher:

The months before my depression started, I thought all was OK with my life. I was working hard at my job and spending a lot of time studying as well. Then I was sitting in a staff meeting and just felt panic – it was like nothing I had ever experienced before. I felt physically sick, sweaty, breathless and hopeless. That was the worst. I suddenly couldn't imagine what I was doing in this job. I was in a dead-end corridor and the lights had gone out.

I was off work for six weeks and went for counselling. One powerful thing I realized was that I really had nothing in my life but work. Yes, I have a long-term girlfriend, but she had never been a priority – which sounds dreadful, but I never gave the relationship much time or energy.

Like Sue, John has realized that 'work' doesn't do it. He needs a balance in his life. Other needs have to be addressed, such as his relationship. His work driver has to be 'turned down' a notch or two.

Try and get the picture of you and your emotions being like a 'car'. Then ask yourself how many people are driving your car? How many people are in your 'car'? How many people do you want in your car? How in control are you? Are you going in the direction that you want or are you just going back to that old 'people-pleasing' driver – 'oh, I don't mind', 'that's okay with me', 'yes, whatever you think,' 'yeh, I'm okay with that,' 'don't worry about me,' 'that's fine', 'I'll go along with whatever you say'. Listen to that – how angry do you feel when you ignore your needs? You are basically negating your own opinions and doing it just to be liked! Don't you realize that people don't respect that sort of behaviour? All they do is take advantage of it. Remember one thing – if you teach people that they can treat you in a certain way, they will. They will do it and they will repeatedly do it until you get so fed up and angry that you react to them, and they will wonder why you are so upset. (You haven't minded before and you've always gone along with it.) Yes, that is probably true. You have always gone along with things because you have been desperately trying to please people, and look what you have got back – pretty much nothing. Well, maybe not nothing. You will have got a lot of grief, anger and very negative feelings. So it is time to stop the people-pleasing, the negativity and the negative self-talk. It is time to come out of that low self-worth.

MOVING FROM NEGATIVE TO POSITIVE

There are so many negative drivers and they are so difficult to identify because they have become a part of your make-up. They have become part of your day and you have simply stopped noticing them. You may say 'this is the way that I am and this is the way that I behave and it is never going to change'. Well, the fact is, it can change, and we think that you will agree with us that it needs to. So let's think about moving some of these negative drivers and replacing them with positive drivers.

You need to get excited at the thought of changing, of becoming the real you, becoming the person you know in your heart of hearts that you could be. Right from this minute, start to get excited about the future. Be optimistic about today in the belief that, for the first time in ages, or maybe the first time ever, you are going to make some positive changes.

This will be the start of a commitment. One day at a time, you will be making some very positive changes in your life, but you are going to make an effort to tell yourself how much you deserve them. People around you are going to get so much delight in you, people who may have suffered because of your negative drivers – your spouse, children, friends, work colleagues, people who care about you, who have watched you and wondered why you have behaved as you have. They have wondered why you can't see all of the good qualities you have, but it is always the way – other people see things that you don't.

This book is all about spotting the things that you haven't been able to see in yourself. The talents, the unused potential, just waiting to be tapped into. Now, don't sit and shake your head while you are reading this and go into that negative driver again, thinking 'this doesn't really apply to me'. Oh yes it does!

Have a look around. How many people are reading this book? Just you. So you need to make your start by looking again at the five steps listed earlier in this chapter on pages 108–9. Then follow these steps:

1 Identify all your negative drivers – make a list of them.
2 Start thinking about all the consequences if you don't.
3 Start replacing them with positive ones – every time you experience that negative feeling coming on, just nip it in the bud. Stop it right there. Remember that it is a learned behaviour. You can learn to reframe this and change it. You are not going to learn to do it overnight, so don't get annoyed with yourself. Don't go falling into that low self-worth driver and say that 'I can't do this', 'I'm not intelligent enough', 'I was obviously born like this'. These reasons are irrelevant; success comes with practice. Remember that continuity breeds success. If you keep doing something, you will get better at it. So get yourself ready for some positive changes in your life. You are in control of this. You are at the steering wheel. It's your driver. It's your car. It's your future and your life. All we are offering you is the 'Challenge to Change' so let's start. Tomorrow really can be different.

SUMMARY

- Drivers can be positive or negative or heavily disguised. Get to know your repertoire and watch out for ones that have swamped others. You must pay attention to balancing the need to achieve and your need for relationships.

- You must take responsibility for yourself and not make excuses.

- Learn to turn negative drivers around. For example, anxiety can be turned into wanting to do something.

- Spotting what is driving you is a useful gauge to measure motives and appropriateness against.

- Set small tasks, or break big ones down, so that you start to complete and achieve.
- Take small risks.
- Get excited!
- Remember that you need close relationships and friends – don't let other drivers push these into the background.

CHAPTER 9

The Change Map

To keep you confidently moving on and making changes, you need to be able to create a map. One that will help you see exactly where you have come from, where you are now and where you are going. It will involve looking at what has and has not worked for you in terms of strategies and goals. This will provide a strong foundation upon which you can safely continue to explore and gain a greater understanding of the process that you will naturally go through. Change is not a linear journey – it is one that has many diversions. You can choose whether these diversions are to affect you positively, by increasing your knowledge and experience, or negatively, by convincing yourself that you can't do it, safe in the knowledge that you have your eye on the final destination and that you won't actually lose your direction. So you can keep your options open, move around the 'change map' and you won't jeopardize yourself in any way.

In business there is the expression 'no plan is a plan to fail' – well, life is a bit like that! How can you get excited enough to take action if you haven't even decided where you are going or feel confident in how you are going to get there? Furthermore, how can you credit yourself with achievements if the goal was never clearly defined? Don't be afraid that you may want to change your goals – they are not to be carved in stone. In fact, your goals will naturally change as you go through life, because what drives you is bound to change. If you stay aware of this and respond to it accordingly you will be experiencing a flexibility that will enhance your life. If you don't, you will end up experiencing unpleasant symptoms, from loss of motivation to serious conditions such as panic attacks, ulcers and depression.

So, as you explore your strategies, several things should happen. First, a picture of what has worked for you should develop. You should also be able to see more clearly how you get stuck, or end up just getting in the way of yourself. The map will thus help you to develop new disciplines of positive behaviour and will give you a very clear picture of where you have come from. Identifying the blocks and diversions will help save you from emotional and motivational crashes. Once you have the picture there is no excuse to stay as you are unless you want to. Remember, most of all, to pay attention to your journey. You need to be aware of the final destination but you also need to allow yourself to enjoy your journey. So don't rush or be impatient – enjoy each part as it unfolds.

A FRAMEWORK FOR YOUR MAP

Here is a framework to help you work on your change map. Bear this in mind as you work on this chapter and indeed on the rest of the book. You don't have to have the answers now. Approach these questions and pointers with flexibility. You don't have to tackle each part in any sequence. Use it instead as a guide that will lead you to 'places' that you may not have intended or realized were a useful part of this journey.

1 Identify Your 'Problem Situations' and Goals

To move further you need to:

1 Be very specific and clear. Generalizations and vagueness will not help you. You need to do this in order to find appropriate strategies and solutions.
2 Be flexible and open. Remember that you are bound to have a perspective but it doesn't have to be the only one. What's more, it is quite likely to lead you straight into self-defeating patterns of thinking and behaving if you are not seeing a way forward. Talking to trusted friends, colleagues or professional helpers will really help you see things from a fresh perspective.
3 Prioritize and be realistic. Don't set yourself up to fail by trying to tackle everything at once. And don't set the impossible. That is sabotage. Break everything down into manageable chunks and take one step at a time.

2 What is it You Want?

1 What are your goals and objectives? To do this you need to have a good understanding of your problem situations and opportunities. This question can be both exciting and frightening. Don't change route because of the challenge of answering this. It is a reality check and it requires you to be honest. Don't de-rail yourself by saying 'I can't answer this'.
2 You need to be able to act on your goals.
3 Get excited and committed enough to do something. Start to think about what rewards and benefits you will experience if you pursue your goal. What are you willing to pay for what you want? Incentives can be improvement in self-esteem, confidence, believing that the problem will be impacted upon positively. The price can be as diverse as taking risks to giving time and energy. Again be clear. You wouldn't buy a car without asking the price. Well, don't embark upon something so important without doing the same.

3 How are You Going to Get There?

What are you going to do? You need to think about:

1. Making a plan.
2. Getting information and advice if you need it.
3. Brainstorming your options and taking your time to select the best one. (It may also be that in time you will think further and come up with more strategies.) Whatever you choose, you must feel capable of using whichever strategy you are comfortable with. Don't copy other people's strategies unless they really are appropriate for you.

4 The Planning Stage

This involves formulating a step-by-step procedure for accomplishing each goal or dealing with a problem scenario.

1. You are more likely to act if you know what you are going to do first and thereafter.
2. Impose time limits.
3. Affirm yourself when you stay on course.
4. Remember to take responsibility.

5 Take Action – Go for it!

1. Talk positively to yourself – get excited, confident and committed, and then act.
2. Do things in stages and keep moving.
3. Remember that the steps are not sequential. So be flexible and fluid.
4. You can set goals and develop strategies or find that new concerns arise while doing this. If so, just back up and do more exploring.

The key is to focus on the final destination by using your change map, but don't be afraid or distracted if it takes you time or you go on some unexpected diversions. The map will always remind you of where you were going.

THE STORY SO FAR

You need to begin by tracing your journey so far. This doesn't have to be done all at once (remember that golden rule of taking things in stages), and we are sure that the end result will be worth every effort. Too many people just want to focus on making changes rather than learning from what has gone before. This is, again, where you can trip up. You cannot just start afresh. You cannot divorce yourself from the past. What's more, there is no need. There is useful information to be taken from mistakes and difficulties – don't waste it. In fact, rather than using words like mistake and problem we want you to start to simply call them EXPERIENCES. Experiences that contain very useful information if you will allow yourself to look, think and digest rather than reacting negatively and either blaming everyone else or being angry with yourself if something has gone wrong. Remember that blame holds you back from taking charge of your life. Think about it. If you are constantly blaming other people, you are not working on yourself. You are also omitting a very important message to yourself that 'you are in charge'. You must take responsibility for today. Believe us, it will serve you well.

The first thing we want you to do is to go back in time as far as you can remember. You need to be able to recall clearly and remember what was going on in your life at that time (you may do this visually, or literally hear or feel what was happening). If this feels very difficult, then work backwards in chunks of time. Often people insist to us that they have bad memories, or don't remember their childhood, and then they astound themselves with the details that they can remember. Yes, it is also important to realize that your memories are bound to be contaminated by what other people have said about your past, but this needn't be a problem. This is unavoidable and you will never be able to separate one from the other. It is important that you put this down on paper and put it into chronological order so that you can refer to it. Once you have worked on this exercise you will naturally find that you remember more and more. So just keep going back and fill in the gaps – write as much or as little as you want. If you want to keep it to dates and brief notes that is okay, or if you want to write more, do that.

Try to think about these key themes.

Dreams and Goals

Can you remember what your dreams and goals were as a young child? Can you remember all the different things that you wanted to be? Some of them may have been more practical than others. Don't be embarrassed – write them down. As you do, can you remember what you were like as you had these first dreams and ambitions? Can you remember really believing that this dream could happen to you?

For how long did you continue to dream? You may even do this today or you may know that there was a break-off point. Which applies to you? Are you still a dreamer or did you make a conscious decision to stop? If you did, why? What had happened or what didn't happen?

How often have you achieved goals and ambitions? Were there milestones in your life where you lost your belief, or did the opposite happen? If there were milestones, you need to look at how you may have linked events that are not actually related. For example, one person we worked with said 'everything was okay until my father died…'. We are not disputing that this was a cataclysmic event in this person's life, but that message and ones like it are very damaging. Just because one very bad thing has happened it does not mean that some trend has been established.

School Days

What are key areas from your school days? Did you enjoy school and do well, or were there problem areas? How did you respond to the goals that were set at school? What sort of messages were you given about your ability to meet goals? What did you say to yourself at this time? (At this stage you may become blocked by remembering other people's goals for you – this is okay – write those down too and what you felt about them and whether you achieved them.)

Expectations of Yourself and Others – Whose Driver is it Anyway?

This is an important area for you to think about. Many of you may feel that your life was actually mapped out by someone else, or that you had to fulfil someone else's ambitions. This is not uncommon. You may come from a family of teachers, doctors, lawyers, etc. You may have an older brother or sister who excelled in a particular subject and you were expected to follow suit – or literally to follow in their footsteps. Or the opposite. You may have come from a non-academic family and, when you showed promise, had the of weight of expectation heaped on you. This is fine if this is the path you want to follow but not if it is really someone else's path, or someone else's map. Or did you, in fact, quite intentionally avoid the family 'map'.

On the other hand, you may not have looked very hard at the future. Perhaps no one sat down with you and encouraged this. You just went along the conveyor belt until it came to an abrupt end and you had to make a quick decision as to where to go next. You may feel that you have never really thought too much about mapping out a future. It may be more a case of you taking whatever has been handed out.

Take Mark for example. He is now in his late 30s and describes himself as 'not doing as well as my contemporaries'. He works with homeless people and 'earns a lot less than everyone I went to college with.' He has friends who are solicitors and bankers and he worries that, although he has a job he enjoys, he may not have fulfilled his career potential. He was a very gifted child. He was particularly good at English and spent hours reading. He had an incredible imagination and dreamed of being on the stage or in films. His parents always steered him towards doing something that would provide him with a secure future but were not specific. They told him that he should choose what he wanted, and that they 'wanted him to be happy'. This was their main goal. For a while, he was top of the class. Because he developed earlier than some of the others, he then suffered because his classmates started to catch him up and he did not deal with the competition very well. He remembers that he didn't respond with any competitive streak and just stopped believing in himself. Each year he was lower and lower down the class, although always in the top 15 per cent. He was also very frightened of exams, and often was surprised by how well or badly he did. He very rarely could predict his results accurately. As a result, he often felt out of control.

When it came to 'choosing' subjects for higher study he still had no real idea of what he wanted to do after school, but he would not consider options that would require higher grades (even though he was capable). He started to develop a strategy, very familiar to many, called AVOIDANCE. This was how he dealt with his lack of confidence. In some ways it worked for him because he was instantly able to reduce his anxious and negative feelings, but it continued to be a very powerful strategy right up to date. As a result, he has paid the price of feeling no improvement in his confidence and feels that he has not achieved what he should have. His self-esteem has plummeted because of this.

We asked him to write out the significant events in his life in chronological order. From avoiding choosing subjects and career options that he was capable of, a chain of avoidance behaviour followed. Incidents that he picked out were as diverse as not asking several girls out because he couldn't bear to be 'turned down', seeing job advertisements and one promotion that he wouldn't apply for, not joining the squash league, and avoiding friends that he considered had done better.

Mark was scared of putting a lot of effort into something and risking failure. If he really wanted something, he would put in a half-hearted effort. It wouldn't matter if he didn't succeed because he would then be able to tell himself that he hadn't tried! He knew what he was doing and did this for a long time but it took a lot for him to own up to it. When he did this it also helped him to look at his cautious, anxious side, or more accurately, the side that steps in and tells him that it won't happen anyway, or that it will go horribly wrong. What a philosophy to live with!

Mark also had to get honest about his drivers. Money had never been a big driver – he is driven (he says it is something to do with his star sign) to help people who are underprivileged and he gets a great deal of satisfaction from doing this. He says he needs to start recognizing this and to stop comparing himself unfavourably to his contemporaries – to stop thinking that he should copy someone else's driver or that it is better than his own.

Key Areas

So, when you look at the key areas in your life, you need to look at your attitude to study, exams, ambitions, career choices, life choices, partnerships, relationships – we have all been there to a greater or lesser degree. What were your messages about ambition? Were your parents very dictatorial about what you should do? Were there pressures to follow in the footsteps of someone? Do you come from a family where lots of the members follow a particular career path? Do you come from a completely different type of family, where you are better educated than your parents and relatives, and therefore have no role models? You also need to establish whether you have ever sat down and asked yourself where you are going, then actually planned to achieve your aims? By planning, you are registering your commitment, which is essential to change, but of course also creates pressures.

DIFFERENT STRATEGIES

There are lots of different strategies for formulating your change map and there are some strategies, such as avoidance, which clearly don't work. Identifying useful strategies will help you get clear about what works for you and will become part of the necessary plan or 'change map'. Before you can do that you need to give up certain unhelpful strategies and learn to turn some around.

The 'Wouldn't it Be Nice' Strategy

Let's take some time to look at a strategy that is almost the direct opposite of the one we have just run through. This one is called the 'wouldn't it be nice if' strategy. Lots of you will recognize this one.

How many of you have led your life so far looking ahead to a picture of something that you are 'hoping' will one day be a reality? There is a world of difference between being optimistic and not living in any reality. This is a bit like the proverbial 'rose-tinted glasses', but it helps to see things more or less for what they are. If you do, you will be better equipped to deal with problems and organize your life. You are also more likely to make things happen because you are being realistic. Remember, if you daydream too much you can confuse your brain into forgetting that something actually hasn't happened. It won't, therefore, continue to work on dreams and goals and come up with any useful strategies or ideas!

The Blank Screen Strategy

There is also the 'blank screen' strategy which is completely negative and destructive. Visual people will say that they 'see' no future. You can turn this around by accepting that you can make use of this lovely blank screen. But keeping it blank won't help you. How can you move forwards when you are moving towards nothing? It's like driving without any headlights. In your mind's eye you need to be 'seeing' where you are going. This way you will find the motivation you need. In fact, it may come more naturally than you would predict.

The Clairvoyant Strategy

There is also the strategy of constantly looking to the future. We call this the 'clairvoyant strategy'. One of the big penalties is that, while you look constantly to the future, you miss out on today. You may also be operating in some blind belief that things will work out. Well, they might, but why not take charge and start making this a reality? People who use this strategy will use phrases like 'it will be great when I get there'. But do they know where 'there' is, and will they recognize it when they arrive at that point?

To help you gain further insight into the strategies you use, go back to an exercise that we asked you to do at the start of the book. It concerned teaching someone to be you! *(See page 10.)* Sit down now and really think about what someone would need to know, and the minute detail that you must tell them so that they could accurately 'act you'. Teach them so that they understand the 'strategies' that you use. Strategies are complex and you must keep checking with yourself as to what happens next, as well as what would happen just before this.

One woman we worked with had a very definite strategy for coping with problems. Say, for example, she received a letter from the Inland Revenue saying that they were making a calculation on her back tax liability. Rather than waiting to see what they computed, she would worry herself to death imagining the worst. This was almost like a superstition. She told herself – if I think the worst it either won't happen or if it does I will at least be prepared. What a way to torture yourself!

Once she worked on this exercise she realized that this strategy was quite a family tradition. She then decided that from now on she will write any worries down and make a map of how to deal with them – she will identify the problem very clearly and then draft some steps that she can take. Part of her map is also about acknowledging what can be done and drawing a line. She also found that she did little forward planning in her life and decided that it would benefit her to develop a greater sense of control.

Think about the things that have influenced you. Do you, for example, have a role model in your family, and do you have lots of messages about what you should and should not do? Do you have your own map or are you really following someone else's or being put off course by what other people do? When you explore the journey so far, what else stands out? Were there things that you were particularly good at? Did you turn out completely differently from what people thought? There are so many instances of successful people reporting how their teachers wrote them off! Or have you had the opposite experience – that people expected a great deal of you but you haven't reached that peak yet? Start to be aware of your unused potential. Also, see if you notice any patterns emerging.

Put the book down now and begin to map out your personal history – detailing your journey so far in chronological order and paying attention to:

1 Identifying patterns.
2 Looking at changes in direction and what facilitated them to happen.
3 Looking at strategies (now that you understand more about what they are). Which ones have you used in your life? You probably weren't aware of what they were. Also, what helped create those strategies or what motivated you to start using them? Have you ever changed strategy?

Having looked back and amassed some information about yourself, we want you to play another game. Picture your 80th birthday party. You are elderly and well-respected in your family. One of your grandchildren asks you to tell them about your journey. WHAT WOULD YOU LIKE TO SAY? If you could write your life history, what would you want it to say? You may be able to be very specific, or you may have certain ideas that don't seem to hang together, but what would you want to say?

CHANGING GOALS AND NEEDS

This leads to the other element of the change map which is understanding that your goals and needs are bound to change and that, for the sake of your mental and physical wellbeing, you must respect this.

Think again about what you need – not always what you want. After all the soul-searching you have been doing, what stands out in terms of what you need?

We recently worked with a very successful, 50-year-old lawyer who was having panic attacks. When he put the physical problem to one side he was able to admit 'I don't want the pressure any more', 'I feel that I need a slower pace', 'the pressure used to suit me and I was excited by the challenge – now it simply makes me feel ill'. This man had the courage to face up to his needs and create a map of change for himself. He was able to see that he needed to address the fact that his 'drivers' had changed. He was in the fast lane of the motorway when he really needed a change of pace.

FURTHER TIPS ON MAP-MAKING

To make your map or plan, you need to understand where you have come from and the influences that you have been exposed to. By understanding these influences and experiences a little better, you will find that you don't have to be the victim of them, unless they really work for you. Continue to be aware of the strategies that you use, be they negative ones like avoidance, or positive ones like creating a sense of excitement by picturing what a situation would be like (almost like a television screen).

Making a map is about assembling a lot of key elements in your life and putting them down in a way that enables you to create the route that you wish to take. You can also plan the diversions that you could safely make as well as identifying the routes that will lead nowhere. To do this you need to think about all the information and insight that you have amassed so far and start to apply it to your goals. You also need to start thinking about where you want to go. If this is difficult, you can often arrive at the answer by asking yourself where you don't want to go! To help you further with this, you need to rethink your drivers – if you are not utilizing your positive ones then you are greatly lacking fuel for the journey ahead.

Sometimes your drivers can conflict. I worked recently with a woman who talked about her two key drivers. One was her job and the other was guilt for not spending time with her husband and children. The end result was depression and anxiety so the map had to be re-examined. She discovered that she had to be prepared to change some things by degree and this helped balance the two conflicting drivers. She also began to realize that these two drivers had been so dominant and had been around such a long time that she had got out of contact with her others. In fact, she wasn't really that aware of them. She also realized that she was not investing her time very wisely – all her self-worth was coming from work and then it was promptly depleted by feeling a bad mother and wife. As well as balancing these two areas, she started to invest in others, and not only did she give more time and energy to her family, but she also started to make contact with friends.

To help you further, here is an example of a change map:

Susan's Map

Here	27, single, secretary, rent a flat.
Short-term goals	Meet Mr Right.
Long-term goals	Children. Live in the country. Have a dog!
Past dreams and goals	To go to university but never did – a huge regret. Marriage, children, happy home.

To be a teacher, but did a secretarial course instead.

When we asked Susan about her dream to go to university and teach, this turned out to be a huge regret. She was always teased about being 'stupid'. She comes from a very academic family. She more or less talked herself out of applying. This was a powerful theme in her life from the age of nine when she wanted to be a Brownie but didn't. She made excuses not to go. After discussing this, she formulated a short-term plan: 'Investigate how I can train to be a teacher. I have nothing to lose!'

SUMMARY

- To move on confidently you need to create your own personalized change map.

- Be clear about where you have come from and list:
  influences in terms of how you have experienced goals, expectations and ambitions;
  where you are now;
  where you are going.

- You need a plan. This is what the map entails but you don't have to be rigid. Take time over it and check your willingness and commitment at each stage.

- Understand which strategies you need to use. Are they effective or do you need to find some new ones? Of course, you can only do this if you are comfortable. (Jo told of a strategy she used to cope with exams which was to make minimum effort so that she would not be afraid of failure. She has since developed new strategies that work better. She has given herself permission to 'have a go' and has learned to be more methodical and change her expectations.)

- Understand what gets in your way and negatively colours your attitude to change.

- Watch out for negative strategies.

- Realize that your drivers will change, and that new experiences will propel you in different directions.

- You should give yourself permission to be flexible and meet challenges and changes of direction as positively as you can.

- The map will remind you of the direction in which you are going so that you can't get lost.

- Take responsibility for yourself and give yourself permission to seek advice and help.

CHAPTER 10

It's An Inside Job

We have talked a lot about why you need to understand 'what drives you' and to learn to differentiate between your positive and negative drivers in particular. In doing this you can start to utilize all your drivers. We have also asked you to start to develop goals – long-term and short-term – as well as becoming aware of any strategies or thought-processes that can put you off-track, such as avoidance and blame, to name just a couple. Team this with the understanding that you must take responsibility for yourself, and you are well armed for the next stage, which is to gain a greater understanding of your needs. This has to be one of your most powerful and fundamental drivers, and strikes at the very essence of your being.

There are many different needs. These can be ranked from the most basic to the more complex:

- Your physiological needs:
  food
  drink
  escape from pain
  sex
  shelter

- Safety
- Attachment and love
- Esteem
- Self-actualization (fulfilling one's potential)

Now we will focus on three major areas:

1 To meet your needs you must first recognize them.
2 There is often a 'tug of war' between the two most powerful needs that you have: relationships and achievements. If this is not clear, then consider the following types of question:

   When you were at school, did you choose subjects because you wanted to do them, or did you choose them to please your parents?
   Have you ever had to decline a promotion that you wanted because it meant spending more time away from home, and your partner objected?
   You also need to be aware of the consequences of making choices according to what you think you OUGHT TO DO rather than according to WHAT IS RIGHT FOR YOU. No matter how successful you might be, you will still be dissatisfied and unhappy because you have ignored a key driver. Remember that when we say 'what is right for you' we are talking at the deepest level.

As you know, the key theme of this book is change. Part of this change is about having the courage to lay aside the drivers which draw or seduce you to make choices at the expense of your needs. If you truly understand and accept your needs and have them at the forefront of your mind, you cannot help but experience a huge change in your life. The change will be internal and quite magical. How often do you see people who seem really happy and content with themselves? There are not a lot of them around but they have such an impact if you have the privilege of meeting them. They exude something that money, status, possessions, education, whatever, will never achieve. This change is about a sense of inner peace and being 'comfortable in your own skin'. This change is about being more in contact with your needs and, as a result, being at one with one of your key 'drivers'.

In contrast, we are sure you can think of people you know who are stuck in the 'tug of war'. (You may well be one of them.) These people may have lots of positives in their lives but they are also restless and dissatisfied souls. They will feel no gratitude for the good things in their lives, and will be constantly striving for what they don't have. These people will be emotionally impoverished. Think of the game of 'is the glass half-full or half-empty?'. There is a world of difference between those who are achieving their needs and therefore truly value what they have, and those poor tormented souls who are the 'half-full' brigade. The most important ingredient that makes one person more likely to be happier than another is that they know themselves well enough to have identified their needs and that they allow themselves to be in contact with that driver. This does not mean that we are encouraging you to ignore others' needs; this is another part of the equation – to respect the needs of those around you and to work towards a compromise.

So, this change has to start from you, from inside you. It is important to look inside yourself in the privacy of your own heart and soul. Really listen to 'yourself', and that means shutting out other voices – they may be voices of your family, or voices from the past. Ask yourself what it is that you need. In other words beware of the 'OUGHT' voice. You also need to differentiate between needs and wants. Go back to the first page of this chapter and review the different levels of needs. Wants operate on a completely different level, and you should always set your needs as the priority, but don't dismiss wants as totally unimportant or irrelevant. You will then have a solid foundation upon which to have some fun with your wants. You may 'want' a high-status job, for example, so that you can have a big house and smart car – but does that fit with what you need? Can you, for example, take the hours and the stress and strain? You know it isn't admitting to failure to say that you don't want to do that – it is about listening to yourself and having the courage to say what it is that you need. By the way, the opposite is also true – if you need status and money, don't be afraid to admit it to yourself but be careful to appreciate that these may not truly fulfil you for long. You may need to learn to strike more of a balance in your life. If you were to do a balance sheet of needs and wants you would find that, if the balance is outweighed by wants, the degree of internal peace will be proportionally reduced, and vice versa.

WHAT IS RIGHT FOR YOU?

Let's now go back to the issue of what is 'right for you'. Here are examples of two men who are driven in opposite ways. As they have identified their needs, they have been able to make some incredibly positive changes.

James is 38 and an advertising executive:

I have always loved being a member of a group. I have great friends and a good family life. I suppose that I like being popular and well thought of.

James then goes on to talk about climbing his particular career ladder:

I used to work for a small advertising company and really enjoyed it. We all worked well together and everyone knew each other well. I am not saying that we didn't argue, but looking back, it was reasonably amicable.

I then decided that I wanted to go further and joined a really huge advertising agency. For a while I liked the challenge. There was a lot of competition between agencies and our clients were very demanding, but I started to feel really unhappy and low and didn't understand why. Now, when I look back, it all started to go wrong when I moved to this agency. I was in a fairly senior position and felt very isolated. I tried going to the pub with colleagues but I realized that, because of my position, I couldn't really be close to people. Also, because it was so much more hierarchical and so much bigger, you could never sort things out face to face. This led to a lot of 'back-biting', which I hated. Worst of all – which might sound quite naive – I realized that people disliked me when I exercised my authority and also envied my success in a really aggressive way. It just dawned on me one day that it just wasn't worth it – I wanted to be able to go to work without a complete dread.

Simon has very different needs. He is 36 and an accountant:

I thrive on personal success – it means a lot to me, but it causes problems in my marriage because I am so career driven. I have recently been promoted in my firm of accountants and I often work until 9.00 and 10.00 and take work home at weekends. My wife feels that my job is more important to me than our family life and is getting really fed up. I just end up feeling angry and guilty, and as a result, I started an affair. That is over now, and I realize that I really do want a relationship, but I also have to have that sense of personal achievement. Since realizing this, I have for the first time spoken to my wife with all the honesty I can muster. She no longer feels shut out but realizes that I have this very powerful driver. I have had to make some compromises, but because we both know that I am compromising she feels a lot more valued (and quite rightly so) and I feel free to pursue my career without feeling guilty when I do have to work late. One of the compromises was to make a real effort to get home earlier, rather than just creating a pattern of working hours that, when I got honest, was not always necessary. It fed my success 'need' at the expense of my relationship, and I do love my wife.

As you have read, Simon and James have very different needs. It does not make one of them better than the other and each one of them has suffered greatly because they were not in contact with their drivers and making them work. They are similar in the way in which they took action as soon as they identified their needs and became honest about them. Neither of them had solutions that were easy to implement, but both of them showed a lot of courage in finding a way forward and understanding that in some areas there had to be a compromise.

The pursuit of money, and how people make their living, is a huge part of everyone's life. Some people may 'over-invest' their time and energy in their work and end up feeling empty because they have simply given too much to this and not developed other areas of their lives or other sources of self-esteem. Someone once said to us that they were concerned for a friend because 'they worshipped the wrong God'. This phrase really had an impact. Again, it is about being careful as to the degree and influence that money has in your life. There is a world of difference between someone who does everything for money and someone who has found the right balance.

We were watching television the other night and an interview really struck us. We watched a very famous rock musician being interviewed about leaving his band. The interviewer asked him how he had been able to cope with giving up his fame and celebrity status. He said that it had been no problem. He went on to say that he felt the reason that the band had enjoyed their success and had stuck together for so long was because they all genuinely loved playing music – the money was not the 'driver' in the beginning. He was also saying that they had been very fortunate because they did something that they really loved and they were very well paid for it. What a combination! If the money had not come into the equation, however, there would still have been a sense of accomplishment and happiness, but if the reverse had happened, the sense of achievement may have been a very hollow and short-lived one.

We all need a sense of purpose, and for that purpose to be as positive as possible it needs to be something that emanates from the innermost part of you. If you operate at this level, that sense of purpose will grow and propel you forwards in an incredibly strong way. It will become an internal energy source that you can tap into. If you never let it get depleted, you will never have to 'run on empty'. This sense of purpose will be fuelled by tapping into your 'needs' and also by opening up your reserves of 'unused' potential.

KEEP A DIARY OF YOUR NEEDS

In order to practise listening to yourself and to gain a greater understanding of your 'needs' we want you to be really honest with yourself and start to keep a diary of how you feel. To help you with this, go back to the list of 'feelings' in Chapter 6 (*see pages 80–1*) and review some of the 'feeling' words. Through a deeper understanding of how you feel you will be able to comprehend your needs much more. If you listen to your needs and keep them uppermost in your decision-making, you will find that elusive sense of purpose and peace.

Keep your private diary over the course of several weeks. Spend as little or as long on it as you like, but do give it some time. Be generous with yourself. This is for you and you need to get into the frame of mind that you are worth giving your time to. Think about that for a moment. As we said at the start of the book, everyone is pressured for time these days, but isn't it nothing less than a tragedy that the last person you devote time to is you? Remember, also, that we are not encouraging you to ignore others' needs, but there has to be a reasonable balance. If you don't tip it a little in your favour, you run a huge risk of being very resentful.

In the previous chapter we asked you to think about making a rather unusual journey – to project yourself to your 80th birthday. Go back to that exercise for a moment, but this time we want you to do something different:

Relax. Put the book down. Shut your eyes and think about whom you would invite to your party. Bring up as much detail as you are comfortable with – don't go any further than that. Picture, though, for a moment, your assembled relatives asking you questions. These are quite specific ones. They are asking you about your journey, about the highlights of your life. The things that have truly made you happy. The things that you would not have missed for the world. What would you want to say? What would delight you? What memories would you want of the people in your life, be they friends, partners or family? If you could choose your path, what things would you need to have happened in your life – big and small?

You may even want to compare this fantasy situation to a real one. You have probably had several milestones in your life already, such as your 18th and 21st birthdays, your wedding, the birth of a first/second child, the list is endless. What did you say about your future during these milestones? What predictions or promises did you make, and how do they fit in with your imaginary 80th celebration?

Go back and look at the work you did on your change map in Chapter 9. Sometimes we have potential and we lose sight of it because it isn't encouraged or it doesn't fit with the grander scheme of things. When we let go of it, a part of us dies with it because we all have capabilities and gifts that are an innate part of us, and to deny them means to deny our very essence. These gifts and capabilities may not always be things that you can build a career on, but that does not make them any less important. Unfortunately, too much emphasis is put on how we make our living rather than taking time to look at ourselves as the complex and fascinating creatures that we are. If, for example, you are very good at art but you have chosen to make your career doing something completely different, do you ever spend any time painting or sculpting? If you have a good voice, do you sing enough? If you are good at needlework, do you spend time doing this? Sadly, the list is endless – and often people will say that they don't have the time.

Nothing can be more priceless than to do something and really enjoy it. In the privacy of our homes, there are many hobbies and interests that people engage in, even though they may not be first class at them. That is not the most important thing. What is most important is that you do something and gain pleasure from it. The two do not have to go hand in hand. In your diary, you may want to keep a note of how many times in the week you have done something purely because you enjoy it. People often want the opportunity to do something very different from what they spend the majority of their time doing. Those in sedentary jobs may be drawn to hard physical sport or gardening, etc. Those whose jobs are more physical may be drawn to doing something less strenuous. We may like our routines and habits as human beings, but we all do well with a little bit of variety – again this helps us explore unused potentials and the rich tapestry which your life should be. It may also be that you have a talent which could well be the springboard for your career, but you haven't had the energy and courage to try it and see.

SUMMARY

- Learn to identify your needs. They are one of the most powerful drivers.

- The 'tug of war' is a really big issue. You have to be prepared to speak to the key people in your life and work towards creating a compromise. Don't shut people out of your life whom you genuinely care about – you will pay a huge price if you do. DON'T SACRIFICE RELATIONSHIPS. Learn that you can resolve these differences no matter how huge they may seem. You don't have to choose one over the other; you have to find a way of making them co-exist.

- Be wary of making choices according to what you think you OUGHT TO DO, rather then according to WHAT IS RIGHT FOR YOU. No matter how successful you might be, you run the risk of being dissatisfied and unhappy.

- We are not encouraging you to hide selfish behaviour behind the cloak of 'getting needs met'. Your needs are fundamental to you whereas your wants are not! Your needs are never selfish – needs are as fundamental as your lungs requiring air.

Consolidating the Change

CHAPTER 11

Am I Good Enough to Feel This Good?

This chapter opens the final section of the book, which is concerned with how to 'empower' yourself. You need to learn to take your power in a healthy and appropriate way as well as ensuring that you aren't literally giving it away, or allowing it to be depleted. We will, therefore, take you through some behaviours and processes that will help you work towards this goal, as well as guarding against the feelings that can wrong-foot you.

You also need to begin to develop your self-esteem or self-worth. If you are to continue to grow and make changes in your life, you need to ensure that you can 'fit' into your success as well as combating others' attempts to derail you. Some people can react very negatively when their friends or family make changes to their lives. This may be because they are jealous, threatened, afraid of losing them or feeling that they are being left behind. So you need to watch out for other people's agendas and not be distracted or dissuaded from the path that you are working on.

Remember, also, that however much you resist change today, you will have naturally made many changes throughout your life already. You therefore have an innate 'blueprint' or ability to accommodate change, if only you let yourself. You cannot and should not stay still –

there are challenges and experiences out there to excite and energize you. To pursue them you need to remind yourself that you are capable and that, most important of all, you deserve that happiness and success. You are worth it, so start acting as if you mean it.

We have already discussed the need for you to take responsibility for your life. This is not said in order to create some sort of impossible burden for you to bear, or for you to think that we are asking you to embark upon some solitary journey. We are speaking of something that is the total opposite – a journey that will bring special rewards if you have the courage to see it through to the end.

THE BLAME TRAP

An important key to moving on in your life is to avoid the 'blame trap'. Don't be lured into it. If you go in there, you will end up wasting time and energy blaming others rather than looking at what you need to do differently. If you don't waste your time and energy blaming or allowing others to blame you unfairly, you are forced to take responsibility for yourself and also make other people in your life do the same. (This does not mean that we are saying don't consider the effect of your behaviour on others, but don't get squashed or derailed by others' blame either.) By taking responsibility, you will become more of the master or mistress of your own destiny and stop being the passenger at that 'bus stop' where all the buses just go sailing by. You will be in charge, empowered and ready for action. If you are busy blaming, you will never be 'in charge'. How could you be? If your attitude is that everyone else causes your problems, the same will apply to your potential good fortune!

Some of you may be reacting strongly to what we have just said about avoiding the 'blame trap'. Perhaps something has happened that has left you feeling perfectly entitled to blame someone, to be very angry and bitter at someone's abusive, cruel, unkind or dishonest behaviour. You are quite likely to be saying 'I did nothing wrong', 'I didn't deserve that'. We don't want you to think that we are disregarding your feelings. What we are suggesting is that you answer this question: 'How many more times are you going to have to pay for someone else's wrong-doing? Really, haven't you suffered enough to know that you need to do something to get free?' Look back to the Introduction where we talked about forgiving. Forgiveness actually sets the victim free. Think about it – if you start to do whatever is necessary to let go of whatever bad thing has happened, you stop allowing an incredibly negative force to live rent-free in your head.

We are not suggesting for a moment that this is easy to do but you will lose nothing by trying to do something. If it feels really bad at the moment, it can't get any worse but it may just start to get better if you take the plunge. There are some exercises in this chapter that will help you, but if you genuinely feel that you cannot cope with this on your own, then get help. That is okay. A lot of people need help to resolve things from the past, and some problems are just too much to try and cope with without professional help. Don't condemn yourself to a lifetime of unnecessary suffering. We have worked with people who have suffered the most appalling tragedies and abuses, and they have found the strength and courage to move on with the support and guidance that they have found in therapy. Some places are just too dark to go into on your own.

Sometimes people can simply put a full stop on the past. This is completely different from ignoring it or putting a layer of emotional concrete on it. You cannot ignore the past or pretend that it hasn't happened, but you can set yourself free. If someone has done something really bad or unkind to you, then you need to 'hand back' the responsibility of the bad behaviour to them. Yes, whatever happened may have left you feeling guilty, ashamed, abused or devalued, but the key thing is that those feelings really don't belong to you! Someone has done something to make you feel this but that negativity is theirs, not yours. The fact that someone has done something very bad to you does not make you a bad person. (Look back again at the Introduction where we talked about the need we all have to understand 'why' things happen. Human beings cannot believe that things just happen out of the blue, so the 'blaming yourself' syndrome is part of you needing to feel, although very perversely, that you have your part in what has happened and are therefore not out of control.) You deserve to free yourself and begin to live your life again as someone who is valuable and deserves good things. The key to your progress is to take that power back symbolically. You may never have to be in contact with whoever hurt you. That may be too dangerous and painful and really isn't necessary, because the start of this process begins the second you make the decision that you are no longer going to be haunted. Eventually you can decrease the space you allocate for these thoughts and refill it with positive things that are happening today.

STEPS TO EMPOWERMENT

There are many areas that you need to work on to give you this important sense of empowerment. Here we will look at shame and guilt, two emotions with the power to distract you and knock you off-track, leaving you feeling unable to cope and unfit for the task ahead. Remember that guilt results from feeling that you have done something wrong, whereas shame is a result of others' actions and gives you the feeling that 'there is something wrong with me'.

For those issues that you feel you can tackle through this book, think about the following:

Making Amends

If you have hurt someone or done something wrong, you could consider trying to make amends. First, though, you need to think of the consequences. Just because you want to say sorry, it does not mean that you will be welcomed with open arms! Think about whether you action may harm yourself or others. If it is a work-related or legal issue, you again need to consider the consequences very carefully. Some of you like this particular game – it is called sabotage because you end up convincing yourself that something bad always has to happen when you try to do something differently. Well, take some responsibility to make it happen – you need to plan and think first!

If you can rectify a situation then go ahead. If not, you will have to consider 'letting go'. Letting go starts with the decision to stop 'holding on' to whatever happened. Stop giving it space in your head. Stop thinking about it and beating yourself up. If you want to do something to let go, write a letter saying the final words on the matter and then find a safe place and burn it to say 'goodbye – it's over now – I need to move on'. Remember that torturing yourself changes nothing. You need to make a decision to move on or stay as you are. The choice is yours. Remember that there is a choice. Guilt is a control that exists to stop human beings repeatedly doing bad or unkind things – if you are truly sorry and have learned by your mistake or wrongdoing, then you need to give yourself permission to move on.

Watch Out for Being Guilted

Watch out for people in your life who feel the need to play on your vulnerabilities and 'guilt you' because they want something from you. Do not get into that game – it is a form of blackmail and you can't afford to keep paying that ransom. What's more, if you respond to 'being guilted', you are simply giving your power away.

Write a Therapeutic Letter

One good exercise with shame and guilt is to write a 'therapeutic letter'. If you cannot personally say sorry because it would cause too much trouble, then write a letter to that person. PLEASE NOTE

THIS IS A LETTER FOR YOUR OWN BENEFIT – DON'T SEND IT TO THE PERSON. Write it as if you were going to give it to them. You will be surprised how good you will feel afterwards. In the same way, you can write to someone who has hurt or shamed you. Tell them exactly what you think of them and end the letter by telling them that they are not going to occupy space in your thoughts any more. The one thing you can actively do to someone who has hurt you is to stop giving them power over you by not thinking about them all the time. They may not know this but you do, and you will feel so much better knowing that you have been able to make this change.

This therapeutic letter can also be very helpful if you are angry with someone. Write the letter, no holds barred, and see how good you feel at the end. Remember, again, that staying angry with someone just gives them a lot of power over you. It is for your benefit to let go of it.

Speaking or 'Praying' to a Higher Power

Sometimes 'praying' in whatever form you are comfortable with really helps. If you are a religious person then this will be particularly meaningful.

Stop Avoiding

If there are situations that frighten you – such as interviews, parties, exams or public speaking – you need to get in charge. Avoiding things, as we have said before, may give your anxiety some temporary relief but the penalties are incredibly high. You will end up losing confidence and giving all your power to situations that you probably could master. As you tackle situations that make you uncomfortable or afraid, remember not to set your expectations too high. Be realistic – set a goal or target that you are likely to attain and then you really can bask in a good dose of glory. So start with situations that would score low on the anxiety scale and keep moving up as you tackle another situation and succeed.

Addictions

If you have an addiction – be it to drugs (prescription or illicit), alcohol, food, gambling, sex, shopping or whatever – you are basically lacking any choice or power in your life. The hallmark of addiction is that it rules you – you don't rule it. When you start, you don't know when you will stop, and when you are not doing it you think a lot about when you will do 'it' next. So whether you are doing it or not, it dominates your life, taking up a lot of space in your head, and leaves you no room for anything or anyone else. Why not consider doing something about this addiction before it ruins you? Get some help for yourself. Have a look at the Resources section (*page 197*) to help you get started.

Take Things One Stage at a Time

Believe that one small step can make a difference. If you cannot see the entire strategy to change or success, don't sit and wait. Get on the move, make some changes and then reassess the next step. As we have said countless times before, you will be surprised by the 'knock-on effect' of making even small changes.

You Don't Need to Wait for a Solution

Don't get stuck in a rut of not doing anything because you cannot see a solution. Perhaps finding a 'solution' is actually not the answer!

Don't Project Wildly

Have you ever noticed that, when you project (think about a future event), it is nearly always negative? So stop doing it, because it just feeds those negative drivers. Also, if you are genuinely worried about something, projecting becomes a form of torture. So stop it and focus on today and the things that you can change. Don't give energy to what can't change.

Get Some Order in Your Life

We are not asking you to become a control freak, but how can you move on if you are constantly in a mess, not able to find things, missing appointments and deadlines? Also, make sure that you take care of your appearance and personal hygiene. In other words, start acting as if you 'can do it' and start looking like you can!

Be Realistic

Give yourself a boost by working on realistic goals, both short-term and long-term. Don't live in a chaotic world of constantly broken promises, unmet deadlines and unfinished tasks. Doing this leaves you feeling bad about yourself and constantly having to apologize to people who are probably bored of hearing it.

Learn New Skills

If there are skills that you lack, don't hold yourself back – go and get them. This may apply in all sorts of areas, from education and hobbies to personal skills.

Be Assertive

Do not confuse assertiveness with being aggressive or selfish – it really is quite different. Being assertive is about getting what you need. You don't need to demand it or be rude. You can find ways of letting those around you know what is okay for you and what isn't.

The keys to being assertive are:

1 Try to be calm when you speak. If you are too angry, then wait.

2 Make sure that the conversation takes place in private and that the other person is likely to be receptive. There is no point in trying to have a conversation if someone is in a rush or distracted.
3 Make your feelings clear without being accusatory, and suggest a course of action or possible solution: 'When you (fill in the action), I feel (fill in the feeling) and I would like it if you could (fill in the suggestion)'. If you have a friend who is always late, you could say: 'When you are late, I feel irritated and I'd prefer if you'd ring because I could get on with something whilst I'm waiting.'

As you suddenly start being assertive, people may react in all sorts of ways. You need to stick to your new path and not be deterred or seek the approval of others. We will look more at this area in Chapter 12.

Reconsult Your Bill of Rights

See page 34.

Avoid Negative Self-talk

You all know what it is, and we have talked before about the need to break it. The only way to do it is to keep challenging it by saying, out loud or silently, the positives. Think about playing a new piece of music. To get it right you have to practise over and over again until you don't have to think about it any more.

So keep practising. Write down the positives and practise replacing the negatives with them. (Also do it when you are more relaxed so that you are prepared.) For example, 'I'm not afraid of speaking in front of crowds. I'm capable'. Try writing statements such as this on cards – pin them up or carry them with you.

FIND YOUR SELF-WORTH

When people take risks and positive things start to happen, they imagine that they should automatically feel better about themselves. However, a lot of people will feel the opposite. Sometimes people can almost have a guilt reaction – do I deserve this?

Here is a checklist for self-worth and self-esteem. Have a look at the list and see how many you can tick. So ask yourself:

1. Do I treat myself well, physically, mentally and spiritually?
2. Can I accept the way I look?
3. Do I take pride in my appearance?
4. Do I eat properly?
5. Do I rest enough?
6. Have I recently been for a medical check-up or to the dentist?
7. Do I respect myself enough not to let others abuse me in any way?
8. Do I like myself?
9. Do I consider myself likeable?
10. Do I believe that I am loveable and deserving of a loving relationship?
11. If I have been rejected by others, do I still believe that I am loveable?
12. Do I associate with emotionally healthy people?
13. Do I accept that if I am in trouble I deserve help and need to ask for it?
14. Do I enjoy my own company?
15. Am I as good to myself as I am to my friends?

16 Do I understand that I don't need to compare myself unfavourably to others?
17 Can I accept my limitations?
18 Can I actually enjoy developing and improving myself rather than beating myself up?
19 Can I sit quietly when being shouted at by someone and accept (if true) that their anger and accusations are actually nothing to do with me?
20 Do I take time to think and act on my needs?
21 Do I take time to experience my sense of spirituality?
22 Do I know that I have a right to be wrong and that I will therefore make mistakes?

As you can see, the list is wide-ranging. Unless you have ticked everything (and this is unlikely), you need to get working on gaining more ticks. There are basic things on the list that you can tackle first.

Dealing with Success

Many children are groomed from an early age not to 'show off' or 'boast', and quite understandably so. But what happens to you if you want success or become successful? A lot of successful people say that they feel isolated and frightened of sharing their success. And those who want to be successful are sometimes scared to admit that this is their goal. There is nothing wrong with wanting success and, more importantly, believing that you deserve it.

Success may be unnerving for another reason. It may mean that you become very different to your family. This can be isolating. It can also make you feel that you are taking a huge step into the unknown. When you are seen to be very successful, people may assume that your life is perfect, and you aren't perceived as having problems. You therefore are unlikely to receive any sympathy or support.

Another problem can be that people won't 'own' their success. Some convince themselves that they are a sort of impostor, waiting to be found out. This is perhaps another reason why people don't see things through – they are scared that it will only be taken away or that there is some sort of humiliation awaiting them. Or that they simply don't deserve to feel this good. Take some time now to think about this, and perhaps write down some of your thoughts and messages.

Beware of Negative Drivers

We spoke earlier on in the book about learning to construct images of what you want and need. Some of you will naturally be very good at this, while less visual people may 'feel' or 'hear' what the scenario would be like. Some of you may be completely blocked by the negative drivers that warn against failure, public shaming, 'getting too big for your boots'. As you propel yourself towards whatever it is you are wanting or needing to do, watch out for these drivers coming into play and literally pushing you backwards. They are not safety nets, as you may once have convinced yourself. They are blocks and hurdles to change that are destructive and negative.

This is such a key point – you have drivers that are supposedly there to protect you, so you avoid doing things because they may pose a risk. This could be a risk of failure or a financial risk. These drivers then come into play, convincing you that you shouldn't do 'whatever', that it is just too risky, when in fact you have to be prepared to take some risks because if you constantly play too safe you will never do anything different.

The next time you are in danger of being driven by negative drivers, just ask yourself one question: 'What evidence do I have that I am heading for disaster?'. If there is evidence, ask yourself: 'Is it **FEAR**?'. Then ask yourself whether there is a possibility that things really can be different this time?

Remember, above everything else, that you deserve success, however great or small and in whatever shape or form – allow yourself that and understand that success will always come as part of a package. Some of it will be very hard to deal with, but don't let difficulties convince you that you haven't done the right thing.

SUMMARY

- Stop giving your power away. You can do this in all sorts of ways and it is time to stop doing it.
- Do some things differently to get empowered, so review the beginning of this chapter.
- If there is anything getting in your way that you can't cope with on your own, then get help.
- Don't make excuses, and avoid the blame trap at all costs.
- Get working on the self-esteem list. Do matter how uncomfortable it feels to work on it – do it.
- Keep challenging the negatives.

CHAPTER 12

Breaking the Patterns

This chapter is about learning to break, or interrupt, unhelpful patterns, to help you achieve a greater state of empowerment. You have already spent quite a lot of time identifying and understanding your patterns; now it is time to start to behave as if you really can make the necessary changes. So you need to stop being a slave to patterns that are unhelpful and potentially destructive. The solution is fairly simple but requires belief, hard work and determination.

You need to understand that, just as patterns can be created, they can also be restructured and changed. So, in a way, the process has to be reversed. You may have 'practised' and 'reinforced' your patterns for years, so it is going to take time to change them, but it can be done. Stop making yourself into some helpless victim of something that clearly does not work and start believing that you can change aspects of yourself that hold you back and are simply unhelpful and disabling. You need to start behaving as if it really is going to happen.

FIND YOUR PATTERNS

You know that you are a creature of habit to some extent, as all human beings are, and it is important to understand how you comfort yourself with the patterns that you have created and followed. They perform two very important functions. First, they give you that important feeling of control and, second, the safety of familiarity. That is fine if the patterns work for you. When they don't, people tend to condemn themselves with messages like 'well, that's just me', 'you can't teach old dogs new tricks'. That is just not true. As you move through your life it makes sense to believe that you will have to find new ways of dealing with situations that may arise and that your repertoire will, therefore, have to be widened accordingly. It may also be that later on in life you gain the confidence to let go of strategies and patterns that just don't work or haven't worked for a long time. You need to watch out, too, for rationalizing your behaviour and therefore justifying a pattern rather than confronting it and admitting that it just doesn't work.

You also need to understand that any change is stressful. It doesn't matter whether you perceive it as being for the better or not. We want you to understand why this happens. Imagine driving in thick snow. If other cars have gone before you there will be a track worn in the snow. If you stay in the groove made by the others, your vehicle will be easier to handle and you just continue on your way. Well, your habits and patterns are a bit like that groove in the snow! Some things feel almost automatic, and when you respond as you always do, it will feel effortless. In fact, you may not even notice what you are doing. So to continue the analogy – if you decide that you are going to drive out of that groove, then some obvious things will happen. The car will become difficult to handle. The journey becomes bumpy and your heart will beat a little faster because you are anxious. You will have to concentrate much harder. Get the idea? So don't be put off by the fact that changing evokes feelings that may be quite uncomfortable – that is natural. Don't see the unpleasant symptoms as a warning sign – they are not.

People also condemn themselves to continue in a pattern because they decide that they must have proof that the 'change' really is going to work, or want a definite formula to follow. Isn't that ridiculous? This is an important 'pattern' in itself, one that requires proof, a blueprint, some guarantee before any new action can happen. There really is no need to be so rigid. Stop saying that 'I am not going to start something unless I know it is going to work'. Change doesn't have to mean 100 per cent, or nothing. You can change by degrees, and this has been a key theme in this book. It really is enough just to decide to make a small start and then see what the effect will be. As you do this, you also need to remember that you have many different patterns of behaviour. You will be conscious of some of these but not others, and many will be greatly influenced by your internal dialogue. One can easily reinforce the other, and it is important to work on all 'patterns' as they are often interrelated and cannot be isolated in terms of impact.

Let's get you to do some exploring now:

1 Choose a 'negative' pattern, but make it a simple one to begin with. Write out each pattern so that, if we were with you, we would know exactly how to 'do' your pattern – be that exact and precise. You have done this type of exercise before, so you really do know what to do.
2 Now identify some positive patterns – really explore them. Again, be so precise about it that we could copy you if we had the information.

To help you, here are some examples of both positive and negative patterns.

Sarah, a 25-year-old secretary, has a pattern that she describes as very positive:

If I have something to do for work, or some sort of a deadline, my approach is always very similar. I will work out how long I need to spend on the task and then write out a plan. I like to do things ahead of time so I make a start as quickly as I can. This is a pattern that I use a great deal for any project, home or work. I have always been like this. I am by nature very methodical and ordered.

Jane, a 35-year-old banker, is the opposite:

I feel that I do my best work when I am 'scared'. I believe that a sense of pressure often produces good work, but as I have climbed the ladder at work and am getting busier, this pattern does not work so well. I am now constantly behind and under pressure and have recently started to make mistakes because I get into such a panic.

George is a 28-year-old personnel officer:

If I have something important to do, such as a big presentation, I like to get myself really well organized. I extend this widely and insist on creating a sense of total order around me. So I will go as far as having my hair cut and choosing the suit I will wear. It's not that I am vain; it just makes me feel better. I will also read extensively (even though I know my subject well). In the lead up to the presentation I will even do things like tidy out a cupboard or attend to correspondence that has been piling up. As a result, I feel very centred and on top of things, well prepared and capable. My mates often laugh at me. They say that I go into these types of situations with 'military precision'. Actually, it feels a bit like that!

James is a teacher in his 30s. He describes himself as a great worrier:

If I am involved in a new project, I always start by thinking about what can go wrong. I tend to do this in all areas of my life. Sometimes this works well because I do some worthwhile trouble-shooting, but in general it gets in my way – I lack spontaneity and am unwilling to take reasonable risks.

Cathy is 27 and a housewife bringing up two children:

I have always struggled with my weight, and have a very familiar pattern with my weight and dieting. I will set a specific goal for my weight loss and make a plan for the diet. I usually plan to diet for three to four months. I feel so disgusted with my weight gain that I want to punish myself. I cut out all foods that I enjoy and really try to stick to boiled fish, green vegetables, hardly any bread or potatoes. I often make it to the end of the target period and then go mad and eat everything that I have missed. I usually end up weighing more than before I dieted.

Tom is 28:

I see a pattern in my relationships. When I meet Ms Right I go completely overboard. I stop seeing my friends and concentrate solely on her. I also get involved really quickly and often feel very possessive and jealous. Nearly every time I have got involved, it is Ms Right that ends the relationship – they all say that it is because I smother them.

Patterns can be like very basic habits. As we said earlier, they can be done without a second's thought and you probably can't initially explain why you do them. Habits can also cover such areas as phobias and obsessions. You may have a fear of spiders or heights, for example. Or you may be obsessive about always sitting in the same carriage on the train or parking in the same spot, or the clothes you wear on a particular day. Some habits may also be linked to superstition. You may, for example, have several rituals which you undertake to stop something bad from happening. A friend once told us that if you see one magpie when you are on your own, you have to salute it, or if you are with someone, you can simply point it out to them. That way you apparently avoid the bad luck that it supposedly brings! Guess what? We have done that ever since! Other 'superstitions' include 'touching wood' and crossing your fingers in an attempt to ward off bad luck. You may well have superstitions that are completely harmless. In that case, leave them be, but if they are getting in the way of your life, you need to do something about them. If you have a severe phobia you may need some professional help to get rid of it (*see Resources, page 197*). Sometimes habits are 'family habits' that have literally been handed down through the generations. They can colour your attitudes to work, the time you get up, the newspaper you read, whether you put the milk in the cup first or the tea – the list can be endless.

Let's now go back to the examples that people have shared with us. First of all, isn't it amazing that so many people can identify and write out examples of their patterns? It doesn't matter if they are only seeing a part of them – it is a start. It is also very striking to see people be so clear about their negative patterns. What does that say? Well, it tells us that many people merrily go on doing something that they know is negative! They have, perhaps, just not been so clear with themselves before. Yes, there will be many reasons why that is the case. You need not fall into getting trapped by what feels familiar.

Look at your first example, your negative pattern. Is your pattern so ingrained that it is almost like a reflex action – you are into it and doing it before you even realize? Looking at your example, what is one of the first things that you do? Is it a piece of internal dialogue, for instance? Have you written that down exactly as it happens? As you know, the things that you say to yourself internally are key points in terms of your drivers. You need to start challenging every piece of internal dialogue that propels you into an unhelpful pattern, as well as keying into any positive things that you say that energize you and help you stay committed. Really continue to work upon your level of awareness. It is awareness that helps get you on the path of making change.

These are the types of questions that you need to ask yourself:

1 What evidence do I have for saying this?
2 When I say that this 'always' happens, do I really mean 'always'? It is important to be specific and honest. Don't be overdramatic!
3 Does this pattern really belong to me or is it more of a family tradition?
4 What would it be like to try a different pattern?
5 What holds me back from trying to do something differently?

Let's work through a couple of examples to illustrate what you need to do:

Carol is 37 and a personnel officer:

I hate doing presentations. When I am asked to do one, I immediately think of how awful I have always felt doing them in the past. I actually go back and feel the feelings as if they are completely real. I perspire, feel sick, get shaky and can't think straight. Then the 'negative voice' chimes in on top: 'You are useless at presentations. I think that Gary who works with me is much better'.

You asked me to answer some questions. This is what I answered:

1. There are several pieces of 'evidence'. I have always been scared of doing presentations, and when I do I really feel ill as I have just described. Well, no actually, that isn't true. The problem started a few years ago – I hadn't thought about that before. All I know is that I get really scared now, and I have messed up more than one presentation because of my nerves.

2. I think I've answered number 2. Well, come to think of it, there definitely was a time when I wasn't so scared. In fact, I was reasonably okay until I came to this company. I hadn't thought about that before – it really feels like it has always been this bad. Something else comes to mind. When I worked for the last company, I had to give presentations to much smaller groups. I think that the combination of my promotion when I came here and the fact that I had to speak to twice as many people made me feel very under pressure.

3. My Dad and brother are excellent public speakers. Funny – the men in the family are – in fact, they often made a point that women were no good at this. My brother used to win competitions at school and Dad was always so proud of him. Mum couldn't do a speech or give a presentation to save her life – in fact, she hates any attention being drawn to her. My Mum has always let Dad have the limelight and leaves a lot of tasks for him to do – oh interesting – I am just thinking about how I do that with Gary – the guy that works with me.

4. Now I've realized a couple of things, I feel that I understand a lot more about what has been happening. I think that I can be clearer with myself from now on. So I will stop saying things like 'always' and I will try to be more positive with myself. I'm actually feeling quite amazed by some of the things that have come out of this exercise.

5. What was holding me back was that I was really telling myself that it couldn't get any better. Now I can think about the times when I was less nervous, and that really helps give me some confidence that things can change.

Go back now to your first example. This is the positive pattern – something you do that works for you. Really look at it again and ask yourself these questions:

1 What is the key that makes this a positive pattern? Again, is this a piece of internal dialogue or do you dwell on previous situations that had a positive outcome? What exactly is it that you do? When you know exactly what it is, you can start to use the information to help you turn some negatives around.

2 Do you know how long you have used this pattern? I wonder if you can trace the origin? This may again prove to be very useful information.

Let's see what Susan does. She is a 20-year-old student who told us:

I have to keep up with my assignment targets. Over time, I have learned not to say that I will do something if I really am not sure that I can achieve it or meet the deadline. This can be from not eating chocolate today, to completing my college assignments on time, to ringing a friend when I said I would. I see myself as an 'all or nothing' person. I try and make this work for me because when it goes the other way I feel a total failure and then want to make everything even worse. My friends often laugh at me because they feel I am on some sort of honesty trip. If they ask me to do something and I am not sure, then I tell them exactly why I can't commit – I suppose that me telling them is as much about me telling myself why I can't as well.

The key for me is the realization of how bad I will feel if I don't keep up – so the reverse is that I think about how good I will feel. When I am on track I feel less panicky and certainly more confident. I like those feelings so I hang on to them!

Remember that you will have strategies that really work for you and others that don't – each time you identify a pattern, take time to stop and examine what it is you do and whether it really is working for you. Use your feelings as a good barometer to what works and what doesn't. Take Susan's example – by listening to herself she knows that making promises or setting targets that are going to end in failure really affect her badly. She therefore deals with several different issues with her pattern. She takes care of herself and maintains her levels of motivation, and she also reaps the benefits of people perceiving her as considerate and committed. For herself, she is also avoiding unnecessary failures because she knows that when she does fail she becomes very sabotaging and her self-esteem gets damaged.

If there are things happening in your life that feel like 'here I go again, this always happens to me' – stop again. You also need to take a look at your part in difficulties. If you continue blaming the situation and blaming everyone else involved, you will never get to learn from your experiences. Again, if there are recurring situations in your life, look at them – learn from them. Don't let problems become patterns, and don't become a passive victim of them – let your positive drivers propel you forward.

'Imagine' what it could be like to do something differently. Imagine the feelings. Imagine the excitement you would feel. Realize that from now on you have more choices than you are in contact with. Just think for a moment of the day that you were born. You had the possibility of living several different 'lives'. Don't ignore that you have choice and don't be afraid of it. Yes, choice can challenge and unsettle you and that is often taken to be a bad sign. People will say 'I didn't pursue it' because it felt so scary and anxiety laden. As we have said so many times before – watch out for that feeling of excitement and don't go labelling it as anxiety.

Start to believe that you can also change patterns in your relationships. Take Natasha for example. She has a difficult relationship with her mother. She sees her mother as very critical of her but still constantly seeks her approval. Their relationship deteriorated steadily over the years. However, things started to change the day Natasha realized that she needed to look elsewhere for affirmation and stopped focusing on her mother – a pattern which existed right up until she was 38 years old. Mum may still not give her what she craves, but their relationship has improved dramatically.

Also, do not oversimplify patterns or ignore the impact that other people will have. We have talked a lot to you about the need for you to take responsibility, but we are not suggesting that you take responsibility for anyone else – you can act appropriately but you must always let others in your life be responsible for themselves. So when it comes to relationships, be very careful about the assumptions that you arrive at regarding patterns. Yes, it is helpful to be aware of 'patterns', but you must also be wary of the fact that there is at least one other person impacting on that pattern. So watch out for how other people's patterns influence and affect you.

SUMMARY

Let's now recap on how you can begin to work on breaking unhelpful patterns:

- If a pattern does not work for you, have the courage to admit it.

- Consider breaking the pattern gradually – one small difference will give you the impetus to move on further.

- Watch out for the negative messages that will constantly come up. Remember that you can change if you want to and have the right help.

- Do consider getting some counselling or therapy support if you feel that you are struggling hard without too much success.

- Don't lump experiences and feelings into one huge insurmountable pile. You will tackle change with greater enthusiasm and energy if there isn't a mountain to climb. So, separate things out and keep them separate. For instance, if you are having problems at work, be specific with yourself. Don't say things like 'this always happens, I never get on with bosses' – be more specific about any pattern. In this example, break the experience down and be accurate – 'I have had problems with some bosses before and I currently don't get on with one of my bosses' – there really is quite a difference when it is put like this, isn't there?

- Don't go to the butcher to buy bread, that is, don't go asking for something from someone who can't give it. This can be a particularly destructive and painful pattern. Look at Natasha's example on page 169.

- Don't project – you are not a clairvoyant! So don't go predicting the future. You obviously need to plan for the future but you don't need to torture yourself over it.

- Start confronting your superstitions and begin to weed out thoughts and beliefs that get in the way of you progressing.

- Stop calling something a pattern when it isn't. 'Oh this is a pattern of mine – everything goes wrong'. Is this type of statement really true?

- Remember that you need to have started to create a new pattern before you can eradicate an old one. Think about the Mum with the dieting problem. Part of the reason that she failed was because she created a temporary pattern that was unpleasant and actually designed as a punishment. It would be much better if she created a plan of eating that could be maintained and become part of a new pattern. If new patterns are not properly installed then it is highly likely that you will simply go back to the old.

CHAPTER 13

Your Soul Survivor

You have already spent a lot of time exploring and getting in contact with what drives you. We now need you to think about that question from a slightly different perspective. We want you to think about what drives you in terms of what would give your life true meaning, a deep sense of belonging, as well as a sense of being truly comfortable in your own skin?

In attempting to answer these types of questions you also need to think about what you believe in. Are you a religious person or do you believe that we are here simply because we are? Or are you a spiritual person? Do you incorporate this into religion, or do you see it as totally different? This chapter is not about telling you what you should believe. It is about helping you utilize an incredible source of power that comes from inside you and can give you the deepest sense of contentment and purpose if you allow yourself to get in contact with it.

WHAT IS SPIRITUALITY?

Spirituality is extremely difficult to define – it's almost like trying to describe a spiral staircase without using your hands! Whatever definitions we have seen always leave us with the feeling that only a small part of it has really been touched upon. We think that one of the best ways to begin to understand is to think of 'it' as whatever enables you to develop the positive and creative part of you. It, therefore, is not necessarily religious, and is not something that you can read a book on and instantaneously factor into your life! This is partly because it is already inside you. It is also so personal and unique to you that the first step to developing it is to recognize that it is there and slowly allow it to emerge in whatever way is meaningful for you. In other words, it is yours – you don't have to emulate other people's ways. Remember at all times that whatever you believe in is fine as long as it works for you. It is very important to have something to believe in, something to hold on to, something to help you survive. Again, we believe that this can be in a religious context or not – your path has to be one that you are comfortable with.

The core of you is your soul or your spirit, an innermost part of you. In this chapter we will look at spirituality as a way of helping you to come to terms with yourself as a human being rather than a human doing. Spirituality will bring you a sense of being connected, a deeper sense of wellbeing, a reason for being, a sense of peace within yourself. We often talk about people being in 'good spirits'; think about what makes you say that about yourself or others. Think also about the expression 'soul-destroying' and the context in which you would use this.

We think that there are many people today who feel a tremendous void and a huge loss of direction in the deepest sense. It is a feeling of the most terrible emptiness. If you have experienced it you will know how frightening and painful it is. People we have worked with have often described a feeling which is like reaching an unexpected 'cross-roads'. The fact that there seems no way forward provokes questions of the most terrifying nature. As a result, they are left wondering where are they going, and why are they doing what they are doing. So people who experience this come to the painful realization that they have simply been existing. That they have been driven in a way that has robbed them of their spirituality, or that other aspects of their lives have dominated to an extent that there has been no time to nurture this. To be in contact again with that inner core you need to stop existing and live. You need above all to stop concentrating on the clutter, the superficial, the meaningless stuff because you will miss out on what you have been given. You will miss out on something incredibly special because spirituality puts you back in contact with who you are and what you need, and acts as a powerful antidote to a life so often driven and dominated by unspiritual things.

By saying that we are not telling you to ignore the practical aspects of your life! You can all recognize being driven by that need to provide a home for yourself and your family, and the need to build some financial security. Just remember that they are not the whole story; they are but a part of what you are about. As people get older they often seek a spiritual meaning in their lives. That may be because they have become disillusioned with other drivers. Or they may feel that they have completed the tasks they set out to achieve and that their other goals are not 'enough' any more. These goals sustain your everyday life but they can do no more than that. You need to be able to reach deeper into yourself to get some spiritual strength. If you don't, you can be left with a deep sense of dissatisfaction. You can end up in a state of emotional and spiritual bankruptcy.

To help you start to find the spiritual side of your life, consider these questions:

- When was the last time you were moved by something beautiful? That could be nature, so it may be a beautiful landscape, flora, fauna, the seasons – the list is endless, or a piece of art, music, poetry, literature or a play you really enjoyed.

- If you are moved by any of these things, ask yourself when was the last time you indulged yourself? How much time do you give to things that really matter to you? We are talking about things that you genuinely love. Things that make you feel 'glad to be alive', privileged to have been able to participate in them, moved, whatever.
- You may also have hobbies and interests that make you feel good. Do you have regular recreational interests or do other things constantly take precedent?
- What about your relationships? Do you take enough time to enrich your spirit by spending time with those who are special to you?

KEYS TO SPIRITUALITY

Having fun is a key to enriching your life spiritually. How you achieve this is going to be very personal, but is an area for you to think about. Fun is not superficial or unnecessary – it is a terribly important thing and needs to be taken seriously!

To lead a life with a healthy degree of spirituality you need to be honest. We don't mean that you should charge around getting yourself into trouble by being blunt or telling people things about you that would leave you vulnerable. What we are talking about is seeking a path that helps you understand yourself more deeply through spending time speaking the truth – being honest with yourself. It will also force you to deal with things that are truly important rather than hiding under the mantle of dishonesty which simply becomes a way of avoiding things that desperately need to change.

You also need to continue to work on areas that cause you to feel guilt and shame. These negative feelings will prevent you from developing your spiritual side to the fullest. In brief, you need to feel good about yourself to really be in contact with spirituality.

Again, you need to tap into the part of you that takes responsibility for your life. It is a key source of power and puts you into the right frame of mind – that you are not a passive actor in your life. As we have often said, you can't control everything and shouldn't wish to, but there are aspects of your life that you have a good deal of control over. When you exercise this choice, you are well on your way to achieving a good sense of spirituality.

What about the important people in your life? People whom you have come to trust and believe in, and people you feel are really there for you and love you unconditionally. Loving and being loved is certainly a very spiritual experience, and a fundamental human need. How much time do you get to spend with family and friends whom you really love and enjoy being with? (Note that we are not speaking about those whose company you don't enjoy!) Good people, people you love and who love you, charge up your spiritual batteries. So spend as much time as you can with those who are dear to you, who bring fun into your life, are inspirational or who may need you.

Have you ever had moments in your life when you have felt truly contented? It could be something as simple as that lovely feeling you have waking up from a Sunday nap, or sunbathing or day-dreaming, to events like seeing your newly born child for the first time. It could be fulfilling an ambition to see a place in the world, or to view a painting that you have admired in a book. Try to think of those moments and make sure that you give yourself opportunities to experience those types of feelings as much as you can.

Are there things that you have always dreamt about doing? We hear so many people saying that they wish they had time to learn how to dance, learn a language, learn how to play a musical instrument. What is it that you have always wanted to do? And why haven't you done it? So often, people don't do things because of fear. Fear stops people experiencing life. To experience spirituality, you need to really live your life and side-step that fear. Stop being afraid of rejection, not being understood, of taking risks. Above all, don't be afraid of doing things differently. Isn't it incredible that so many people can acknowledge an emptiness in their lives and then do nothing? Sadly, it is often those negative voices that say that nothing can be different that actually hold them back. So some people end up living in self-imposed prisons. Believe from this moment on that you don't have to stay inside – take responsibility for your happiness and mental wellbeing and you will find spirituality.

Are you constantly battling with time? Again, it is very difficult to charge up the spiritual batteries if you are always exhausted and never have time for yourself. If you are working too hard – be it with an occupation, bringing up a family, or nursing someone – how many times do you ask yourself whether your tiredness is unavoidable? Never accept exhaustion as being totally inevitable and something that cannot be changed. There may be small things that you can do to alleviate some of it, and in turn you then open up time for the spiritual side of you. When you are stretched, be careful not to take on further tasks when you don't need to. Also, don't set yourself impossible targets – that just pushes you into a spiral of failure and probably having to let other people down. Remember that never having 'time' does not fit with leading a spiritual life. We looked up the word 'spirit' in the dictionary – it said 'the force that animates the body' – see what we mean? How can you be spiritual if you are exhausted? The answer is that you can't, and the sad thing is that you are slowly killing off the thing that is so vital, so important, and something that you literally can't live without.

Some of you may have moved away from the religion you were brought up with. You may never return to it, but there may be some of you who feel a sense of loss. Or perhaps you have been drawn to pursuing a different one. We asked you once before to play the game of projecting yourself forward to your 80th birthday party (*see page 130*). It is useful to do this again now. Think about what you would really like from your life. Again, there will be material requirements – we understand that – but what else do you need? Take some time now to think about why people seek a more spiritual, or religious, path or really 'down-shift' their lives. Could it be that they reach a realization that what they have does not fulfil them, that what they have may even be getting in the way or holding them back from finding some inner happiness that they know they really need?

Remember that you are your 'soul survivor'. You, and only you, have got the keys to giving yourself this inner peace which is attainable if you let it happen. We have talked a lot about you taking responsibility – here is another area that you will miss out on if you don't make it happen. You can't wait for someone or something to happen to create the catalyst – it can begin with a decision and will never stop once you have set it in motion. Yes, you could probably throw back a lot of excuses as to why you can't have this or why you don't deserve it, why other people can attain it but you can't. You need to continue to confront the part of you that does this. Remember that nothing breaks habit like habit. Let's say it again. Nothing breaks habit like habit. Now is the time to start getting in the way of those old negative behaviours, that disabling self-talk that you have continually been listening to. You have fallen into this very bad habit of telling yourself that it is okay for everyone else but it is not okay for you. Watch out for this behaviour because it alienates you from any spiritual path, let alone spiritual growth.

If you are sitting reading this and feel stuck with 'spiritual equals religious', or that it involves some wacky belief or behaviour – stop now! Don't block yourself unnecessarily. Religion and spirituality are completely different, and if you read this chapter carefully you will see that. You will also be well aware that we are not suggesting any weird or strange rituals or practices! The key thing is that you have to be you in order to be spiritual. That is the point. That is why people that play-act at being spiritual stand out – because they are not being honest. Try and remember the last time you met someone with a feeling of peace and contentment around them. Can you remember how that felt? Can you remember thinking 'I'd like some of that – I wonder how they have got to be like that'?

From this moment onwards, it is time to open yourself to yourself and not be held back by redundant behaviours and habits. Let yourself start to feel who you really are. This may feel frightening, but think about the rewards. Remember that spiritual emptiness is almost invariably filled with negative feelings that are not true. Sadly, because you have been feeling them for so long, you will have started to believe them. You have started to tell yourself that they are true, that you can't change them – no matter how much you try. Well, this time it is going to be different.

Have you ever noticed what happens when you 'try' to do something? You never really get there, do you? **T R Y** stands for 'Today Repeating Yesterday'. So trying isn't the answer – it doesn't work. The answer is to 'do'. You've got to take your 'soul survivor' and gel it with the person you are today. That is what is going to give you the strength to gather some spirituality around you. Your 'soul survivor' is that part of you that does and always will cope and survive. Yes, no matter how 'battle weary' and scarred you may be, you have survived. You are still here today. Yes, you may feel negative. Yes, you may feel empty. Yes, you may feel all those feelings of worthlessness, low self-esteem, loneliness and isolation, but you have survived! You have managed to come through the traumas and difficulties of your journey through life. If you can survive all this, just think of how much you can do with a positive sense of self around you. In the end, you will break that old myth of those feelings only belonging to other people and not to you. You have a right to your happiness, to have good feelings about yourself. You have a right to change, but without spirituality in your life there will always be that void – that feeling of emptiness.

As we have said before, spirituality is hard to define because it is such an individual and personal experience, but the main components are a sense of wellbeing, a feeling of being able to sit down and just look out of your window and feel as if you are part of something – not all of it, not the master of it, not in charge of it, but just a part of it. Spirituality is an acceptance of who we are and of our limitations. It is knowledge that we can't do everything, but also an awareness of the things we know we can do well, for which we are grateful. So be grateful for your soul survivor. Be grateful for that part of you that has a sense of purpose and a direction. In time you will move closer to the part of you that can attain that feeling of wholeness and peacefulness within yourself.

So spirituality is about feeling good enough to be you. It is both an energy source and the place where self-esteem can spring from. It gives you a sense of goodness and wellbeing – that life is meaningful and you really do belong. It is, as we have said before, almost like an antidote to the negatives that modern life constantly throws at you, and if you work on developing this area in whatever way is meaningful and helpful to you, you will benefit tremendously. It will create the sense of direction that you naturally crave, and if you really listen to yourself you will start to truly realize your potential. So start to push yourself in the direction of spiritual wellness and awareness.

It's okay if you haven't thought about spirituality before reading this book. That is nothing to be ashamed of. The whole experience of this book is to help you change and to feel better about yourself. The only way this can happen is by deciding to make that start now. You are your soul survivor. You are the one in charge of this. You are the only one who can make the changes. We can only make suggestions and support you in your positive decision to change your outlook. With all this potential, don't you think it would be a huge mistake not to use it in your quest for inner peace which you deserve? Realize now that it is only by tackling problems that you grow mentally and spiritually. It is only because of fear that a lot of you will have avoided moving forwards but now you are beginning to understand that fear is simply 'false evidence' – it really is not so frightening.

So remember above all else that a life enhanced by spirituality creates an opportunity to balance those somewhat opposing forces of freedom and dependence, the struggle between your drive to achieve and your relationships, your wants and your needs. It is the basis of self-worth and the key to empowerment, and is inside you if only you use the key and find out.

The path to finding it may be very simple. It may literally be taking the opportunity to be quiet and to think (not necessarily meditate). It may be going to, or creating, a special place. You may want to make a little sanctuary in your garden, or in the corner of your bedroom. You may choose special books, music, art, whatever that inspires you. You may make a promise to take some time each day to be with a loved one – not just the day-to-day being with someone but actually being with them and making the time special. The possibilities are endless.

SUMMARY

- Spirituality is complex and difficult to explain but the best place to start is that it is whatever enables and develops positive and creative forces in a human being. It is also something that gives your life meaning and you a sense of belonging.

- Don't confuse it with religion – it is something quite different. If you are not a religious person it does not prevent you from being a spiritual one, and vice versa.

- Seek and develop your sense of spirituality in a unique and personal way – doing this will make it feel completely right and meaningful for you rather than trying to follow someone else's blueprint.

- You are likely to need a spiritual boost if you are currently experiencing a loss of direction in your life, the feeling of being at an uncomfortable crossroads.

- It is not wacky or impractical. You need to attend to the practical side of your life as well as the spiritual – they are both important.

- Think about the areas in your life that evoke feelings of wonder and peace – they may be things like music, art, nature, relationships – the list is endless and again very personal but the key question to ask yourself is 'how much time am I giving to these areas?'.

- That leads us on to reminding you that time is the greatest enemy of spirituality. How can you be spiritual when your are exhausted and give no time to anything but work (be it inside or outside the home)?

- Watch out for spiritual emptiness being filled with negative feelings. Conversely, if you are 'filled up' spiritually then there is less room for the negatives.

- Spirituality is the antidote to the negatives modern-day life throws at you.

CHAPTER 14

Instant Access to Peace and Readiness

You have now reached the final chapter of the book so we will take a little time with you to reassess your journey so far. In doing so, we will draw together the different strands of the book. The main part of this chapter will, however, focus you on beginning to learn to create and access a state of mind that can help provide a greater sense of peace – from this will also eventually come a state of readiness and confidence. It will take practice and patience, but if you work hard at it, you will reap the rewards that you deserve.

By working on the exercises in the book you will have started to achieve a greater degree of understanding and insight, but insight is of absolutely no use unless you do something with it! By now, you will have begun to achieve a state of mind that enables you to see things differently, which will in turn directly impact on how you are feeling. You will have started to confront whatever you feel needs to change, and by utilizing some of the techniques illustrated in this book, you will have felt confident enough to move on to the action stage, pacing yourself in a way that is appropriate for you. Your explorations will have created that 'window of opportunity'. This time, however, you have not only created it, but you have opened it as well and passed through to the other side, rather than creating it and turning your back as if it never existed. In the past, this will have left you with the frustration of seeing what can be different but never taking up that challenge. Each time this has happened it will have eroded your confidence that things can change – you are stuck in that self-fulfilling prophecy, believing it to be completely true. So by implementing certain changes you have created that necessary antidote. As a result, you will be well on your way to achieving a tremendous sense of empowerment. Not only have you made some changes, you have maintained them too, and as a result you will feel more confident to tackle others. That success will drive you forward because it creates an energy source and a state of mind that makes it all feel possible. It is in this state that some dreams can actually become reality.

The final phase, which comes from all of this hard work, is finding that true, deeper sense of peace. By clearing away some of the debris and clutter, the way forward seems clearer and simpler, and looking back will feel more comfortable. Whatever lies in your past, you now realize that you have a choice as to the impact it has on you today. You are also fully aware that if you are still struggling with it, you deserve to get help – however long you have to work at getting free, the end result will be really worth it. We don't underestimate the difficulties that you may have, but that does not stop us from telling you that you can get free with the right help.

Let's now go back and think about some of the themes that have been covered throughout the book. While working on the book you may have begun to experience some of the following. (You may want to add to this list – these are just a few for you to consider while you are recapping.)

- The feeling that you are wading through obstacles or dragging your past with you has diminished.

- You feel a greater sense of freedom.
- You will be more aware of choices.
- You no longer confuse excitement with anxiety, and as a result feel more willing and able to take up challenges.
- You appreciate that change is difficult and stressful – whether you perceive the change to be negative or positive.
- You set achievable targets, and each time you succeed you move the goal a little further along, if necessary.
- You break tasks and goals down into manageable chunks. You no longer build that mountain and feel exhausted at the prospect of 'climbing' it.
- You will not be projecting so negatively into the future.
- Your negative inner voice will be quieter.
- You will not make so many inaccurate generalizations that will damage your motivation and drive.
- You will not go shopping at the butchers to buy bread! (If you don't understand this comment then look back to Chapter 12.)
- You are more in contact with your needs and are allowing them to drive you.
- You also understand that there is a natural 'tug of war' between pleasing those whom you love and meeting your own needs.
- You understand that solving problems in relationships does not require a black-and-white solution and that there has to be compromise.
- You are more honest about what drives you.
- You are more in contact with other positive drivers and alerted to your negative ones.

- You have started to develop a greater sense of spirituality, or at least are more in contact with it.
- You are aware of 'patterns' and now understand that you don't have to be a helpless victim of them if they don't work for you.
- You believe that you can change even if you are not totally sure how to!
- You are taking responsibility for yourself in the healthiest way. You are now a lot clearer that relationships are about each individual contributing their 50 per cent, and that successful relationships are created by communication and negotiation.

FINDING INSTANT PEACE

Let's move on now and look at the techniques for achieving an immediate state of peacefulness or readiness – as instant as putting a bank card into the 'hole in the wall' and retrieving money! Peacefulness is different to relaxation – it is a state of good self-esteem, confidence and drive (not a stressful one – one that just lets you know that you know where you are going). Think about the expression a tennis player wears as he prepares to serve, or the athlete on the starting block – all these people know where they are going and they know what to do. Their hearts may beat a little faster but it will be accompanied by an inner sense of calm (just look at the composed expression on their faces). As they are on the starting block or throwing the ball into the air, they will be telling themselves that 'they can do it', and what's more, they know that they can.

Put the book down and just try and imagine that feeling for a couple of minutes – think about a particular task and make it one that poses a degree of challenge for you. It may be a speech, a presentation, a confrontation with someone, taking a faulty item back to a shop, whatever. Imagine yourself on the brink of starting that task, and will yourself into a sense of 'I can do it', 'it is going to be okay'.

What do you need to do to get into the frame of mind that you 'can do it'? What do you think about? What do you picture? What words or phrases do you hear? Do you think about other times in your life when you have succeeded in a difficult or stressful situation?

To help you think more about this, let's take Jessica as an example. She is a relationships counsellor and was asked to appear on a daytime television chat show. This is what she did to turn her nervousness around:

I really wanted to do the programme but was very nervous about it. I'd never done television before and didn't want to make a fool of myself or let my organization down. When it came to the day I was due to appear, I stood in the corridor of the studio minutes before going on and was feeling really sick, nervous, sweaty and shaky. If I wasn't dashing backwards and forwards to the loo, I literally stood there quaking and obsessed with how nervous I was. I decided there and then that I had to do something because I felt terrible. I actually felt convinced that I had made a terrible mistake and that I wasn't capable – in fact, I thought I would collapse at one point! I really am not exaggerating. I physically felt dreadful and I couldn't think straight.

At some stage I thought 'this is crazy'. I actually knew I couldn't go on in the state that I was in so I had to do something. I asked myself why I was so nervous. I ignored the negative answers because I was well in contact with them anyway – I didn't need to reinforce them. The 'positive' voice responded that it was because I wanted to do well. I immediately felt a bit different – yes – I wanted it to be a success and I began to imagine what it would feel like coming off the set if I had done well.

I then felt a faint glimmer of excitement, and bit by bit the nervousness was transformed. From then on I kept reminding myself that I was excited and I just wanted to do well. From that point on I stopped labelling my feelings as nervousness and just tried to stay as positive as I could. In fact, at one point I kept reciting in this manic way that 'I am so excited – gracious, I am so excited...'. I then thought about other times in my life when I had done things well under stressful situations, and one thing just seemed to reinforce the other. The next moment I was called on to the set and, yes, I was still nervous but it wasn't disabling and I did well.

Think about the different rituals athletes and sports people have. Some rituals are loud and appear aggressive, such as those of the All Blacks rugby team. Others are more silent and passive, but the end result is that these rituals instantly change the way you feel because as that ritual is repeated and perfected, the more powerful it becomes. There are many different ways to achieve this mood. It may be, for example, that you have a piece of music that helps you change how you feel. It may be an instrumental piece or it may be an upbeat pop song with lyrics that really stir you into action. If it works, use it! It may be that before you do something challenging or difficult you take time to build a 'story' or 'script' reminding you of your strengths and abilities and past times when you have succeeded, and you use that to give you the confidence to 'do it'.

Other people have quite 'superstitious' types of rituals. We have worked with one man who has a 'lucky' jacket. The first time he did a presentation he wore this jacket and it went well. He therefore attributed 'luck' to this garment. He has worn it ever since. It doesn't matter whether you really believe that a garment can be lucky. That is actually irrelevant. The key thing for this man is the fact that his mood changes when he puts on this jacket because it makes him 'feel lucky'. Thus, he chooses his mood and simply utilizes the jacket to reinforce it. It is exactly the same with other rituals. The ritual itself may almost be insignificant but the key thing is that the person is making the choice to feel different and the ritual is seen to help them achieve this. As the ritual and the positive outcome continue to be linked and therefore reinforced, the more powerful the effect, so that as soon as a person begins their particular ritual, the positive feelings will start to flow.

Strangely enough, the day we were working on this chapter we saw someone who had found their instant access to peace and confidence in the most magical way:

The day had started terribly badly. I was feeling really wound up and depressed. I had wanted to go to this art exhibition for ages but that day I just wanted to forget about it. I felt scared of going out and that something really bad would happen if I did. Well, luck had it that Tom, my partner, remembered the exhibition was on and insisted that we went. I was in such a state – I tried to dissuade him and he just said 'look, we'll go, and if you really feel bad we can come home'. I thought I could still get out of it because there is usually a huge problem with parking around there. Well, guess what? There was a space right outside the exhibition when we arrived. That made me laugh but I didn't feel any more optimistic – it felt more like a conspiracy, and I felt really sick as I walked up the steps and saw all the people in there.

Anyway, we went in and I started to relax. There were so many beautiful paintings that I became totally engrossed in them and stayed for over two hours. During this time I saw a painting, fell in love with it and bought it. To cut a long story short, it has become my 'instant access to peace'. I love the painting – I think that it is so beautiful and intriguing, but even more, it just makes me immediately feel good every time I look at it. It reminds me of a day that was completely turned around, and each time I look at it I instantly think of how good I felt when I saw it and those good feelings just flood back. Last night I walked home for the first time since it was hung – the light was on above it and I saw the painting from the street. I just smiled and felt really happy.

RESOURCES FOR PEACE AND CONFIDENCE

Let's now recap a little bit more and look more broadly at the resources you need to tap into in order to achieve this state of peace and confidence, as well as watching out for the blocks that will simply get in your way:

A Greater Understanding of Yourself

Knowing your positives and negatives, and allowing yourself those negatives. You can't be good at everything, and not everything can or should always go right. Make sure, though, that you really know your positives – don't be one of those people who hide behind a false modesty and just get left behind.

Know Where You are Going

You have made some decisions for the future and this forms a game plan which will be both motivating and reassuring. Again, think of the tennis player and athlete. You can face tests when you know what to do, you know why you are doing it, you know what direction it will take and, most important of all, you believe that you have the capabilities to do it and the inner strength to withstand any negative drivers. Think of soldiers going into battle. Have you ever asked yourself how they can do it? The big factors are their training and preparation. Some of their natural fear is diluted because they have a tight plan which has been rehearsed and they have a sequence of movements to follow. They too have to allow for the unpredictable but they at least start from a solid foundation.

Just simply knowing where you are going is a 'state' in itself. There lies a sense of safety and security. You are not attempting to predict the future but you are armed with the decision that you have made and you have given yourself permission to 'have a go'. You will also have a sense of contentment because you have began to address that it is not necessary to do things perfectly. You have begun to realize that it is okay to do your best, and this will allow you to take pleasure in the participation, and not stress yourself unduly with the achievement driver.

No Longer Being Afraid of Making Mistakes

Giving yourself permission to make mistakes and not beating yourself up. This notion will be alien to a large number of you – but just think for one moment what it would be like to be comfortable with making mistakes. It looks strange written down like that, doesn't it? But what a wonderful thought that you could actually stop tormenting yourself and start to see mistakes as experiences that you can at least learn from. You might also like to consider dropping the word failure from your vocabulary. It is such a damning word and so negative. Yes, we know it looks simple on paper. There probably are experiences that you could simply do without and you don't feel that there is anything to gain from them. Don't get distracted by those – that's not what we are referring to. We are talking about the things that can be changed – the things over which you do have some power. Don't get caught up in what can't be changed – you know what these things are. Stop getting blocked by them.

Abstain from Perfectionism

It isn't a laudable state. It is a state of mind that creates no opportunity for ever feeling true achievement – because you simply can never do things perfectly. It also stops you from doing things because you assess whether you can do them perfectly, and if you can't you tell yourself there is no point in continuing. Be careful that this has not been masquerading in your life as a positive driver because it isn't – really start to watch out for this.

Playing the Good Fortune Lottery

What drives you to believe that there is a lottery for good fortune and that the winning ticket is just never bought by you but by other people? 'Why shouldn't good things happen to me?' We know that you can dwell on your 'bad luck' and feel anxious that, if you have had some, you are bound to have some more. Some people can also convince themselves that worrying is almost like an antidote to problems – 'if I worry myself sick about something, it actually won't happen'. But while people are busy protecting themselves in this negative way they are paying a very heavy price because the negative drivers are in charge. While you are in the grip of the negative drivers, nothing positive can happen. This is almost like some superstitious ritual or bargaining device – 'if I torment myself with worry, things will be okay'. Do you recognize this one?

Look at Your Talents

Take time to think about the things you are good at – take time to consider the thought processes that accompany them. What is it you do so that there is a positive or successful outcome? You need to feel that you sometimes can control an outcome. Really continue to work on identifying useful strategies, and allow yourself to believe that there is a healthy degree of control – but don't imagine for one second that we are encouraging you to become a control freak! Neither will we ever encourage you to believe that you can control the uncontrollable – you can't, and it is very healthy to realize that you can't control people, places or things! You may be able to exert an influence, but even then don't get lured into believing that you have that amount of power.

New Drivers

Think about developing some new drivers such as:

- Enjoyment
- Exploration
- Excitement
- Peace

Stop Doing 'Guilt'

We are not asking you not to have morals or respond to duties and responsibilities. What we are asking you to do is to stop being driven by guilt. If you let it get a big hold, its power will grow and grow. It is the cause of much torment, unhappiness and depression.

You need to make a decision. If you feel guilty about something then you must either try to do something about it or let go of it. If, for example, you are torn between work commitments and family and you are being pulled in two different directions, you need to do something. Don't stay in the guilt – it will destroy you. Look back to previous chapters where we have talked more deeply about this.

Your Personal Programme

You need to find your own personal way of imprinting all of this so that you can access it at a moment's notice – somewhat like putting a disc of information into a computer. It may be that the good feelings that come from working on this section can be triggered by associating them with something like a poem, a piece of music, a scene from nature, a very treasured memory, or whatever is meaningful for you. Sit down when you can and consider how you are going to achieve this. A friend of ours gave us their example:

I have this magic chair that I imagine. So when I sit down on any chair I tell myself that I am sinking into this chair. I know the feel of its soft cushions, even the smell of the fabric. The chair is very nurturing and lets my positive voice become free. So as I sit down the voice starts and begins to tell me all the positive things I need to know in order to tackle whatever difficult task lies ahead. I just literally bask in this chair until I feel ready for whatever it is that I need to do.

Forgiveness

We have talked on several occasions about forgiveness. The fact that it keeps reappearing shows how important this is. It is especially important when it comes to developing a sense of peace. Remember, we are not talking about you necessarily forgiving someone in order to make them feel better – the most important thing to understand about forgiveness is that it makes you feel better. It is something that sets you free. When you forgive you can actually stop having to think about whatever happened and you can start to move on. Remember that we are not saying that people can completely forget – that would be ridiculous – but you can move on. By doing so, you can create some distance which softens bad memories, and in time that memory can 'fade'.

You also need to think about forgiving yourself. It may be that you have done something that has hurt someone else or done something illegal or wrong. It may be that you made a decision that turned out to have terrible implications. Again, you cannot move on until you forgive, and not forgiving simply means that you condemn yourself to being punished forever.

Letting Go

This follows on from forgiveness. Every time you dwell on something negative that someone else has done, or you dwell on your own mistakes, you are trapping yourself in something that has gone. The moment or experience is over; the feelings about it may live on – that is the problem. Also, yes, there may be consequences that have an impact today. So what can you do? You may have to put up with the consequences, but you can do something about the feelings.

Acceptance

Sometimes damage cannot be undone – but you don't have to reinforce it and continue to pay the price for the rest of your life. Realize now that every time you think about something negative you continue to give your energy and time to it. If you can accept and let go, you will become free.

Powerlessness

Some of you reading this may be familiar with the '12 step programme' of Alcoholics Anonymous. One of the masterpieces in its philosophy is the concept of 'Powerlessness'. Most people fight that feeling, but peace comes from accepting that we are genuinely powerless over people, places and things. In other words, stop trying to control the uncontrollable – life will be less painful and stressful when you do. Don't waste energy or serenity where things cannot be changed or controlled. By all means, spend it on the parts of your life that can be influenced, but don't throw your sanity and wellbeing away on things that cannot be changed.

What is the Value of what I am Doing?

Ask yourself this question. In other words, make sure that you check out with yourself what exactly you get out of doing whatever it is that you do. Keep asking this question and you may end up with many surprises!

If you continue working on all of these areas you will find that you become increasingly in contact with your positive drivers. You will also find that you are stopping doing things that simply don't work or, at worst, actually create problems for you in terms of making you feel hopeless, anxious, depressed, angry or whatever. To create your own 'instant access to peace' you need to explore what will work for you. Remember that you are unique and it is important to take the time to find what works for you personally. Once you have decided, you need to work at it on a frequent basis. This will eventually allow you to 'tune' straight in and just bask in the wonderful, positive feelings that will come. So it may be a piece of music, a 'magic' jacket or chair, a painting, a spectacular view – it doesn't matter – you choose and make it work for you. There may be some uphill climbs ahead of you but just take it one step at a time and remember to carry that 'instant access' with you at all times.

You may have reached the end of this book but this is just the beginning of your journey of change. Well done for having the courage and openness to start this journey. If you have taken the time to read all of the book, do the assignments and exercises, you will be armed with information and ideas that will help you continue to develop and increase your levels of motivation and make the challenge of change something that can be a healthy and exciting part of your life rather than a fantasy that never comes to fruition. Start to believe that it is possible, silence those negative voices that hold you back, and really get to understand those drivers that will naturally propel you forwards. You have nothing to lose and probably more to gain than you will ever imagine. Believe, above all else, that you truly deserve the good things that will happen to you, and let yourself be excited by that thought.

RESOURCES

Here are a few telephone numbers and books to help you further:

ALCOHOL PROBLEMS

Alcoholics Anonymous
Helpline: 0171–833 0022
This organization has excellent literature.

Al-Anon
Helpline: 0171–403 0888
For families and friends of alcoholics.

Book
The Effective Way To Stop Drinking, Beechy Colclough

EATING DISORDERS

Overeaters Anonymous
Helpline: (01426) 984674
This organization has excellent literature.

Eating Disorders Association
Adult helpline: (01603) 621414
(Open 9am to 6.30pm, Monday to Friday.)
Helpline for 18 years and under only: (01603) 765050
Open 4pm to 6pm, Monday to Friday

Book

It's Not What You Eat It's Why You Eat It, Beechy Colclough

DRUG PROBLEMS

Narcotics Anonymous

Helpline: 0171–730 0009

Families Anonymous

Helpline: 0171–498 4680

For families and friends of addicts.

GAMBLING PROBLEMS

Gamblers Anonymous

Helpline: 0171–384 3040

COUNSELLORS AND THERAPISTS

If you want to find a counsellor or therapist, there are several ways to find the right person for you:

1 Through personal recommendation.
2 Through your general practitioner – you may even find that they have one at your surgery.
3 Contact the British Association of Counselling for their list on (01788) 578328.

MENTAL HEALTH

Book

Understanding Obsessions and Compulsions, Dr Frank Tallis, Sheldon Press

www.thorsons.com